ETHICS, GOVERNANCE AND CORPORATE SOCIAL RESPONSIBILITY IN INDIA

Issues and Perspectives

The Rt Hon The Lord Rana, Baron of Malone Member House of Lords—British Parliament—London

Lord Diljit Rana is a successful businessman in Belfast, Northern Ireland. He is Chairman and Chief Executive of Andras House Group, Northern Ireland's biggest hotels and hospitality organisation. Born at Sanghol in Punjab, Lord Rana has lived in Northern Ireland since 1966.

His achievements are listed below:

- He was appointed to the House of Lords in 2004 by the then UK Prime Minister Tony Blair in recognition of his work in driving the successful regeneration of Belfast city centre and his efforts to encourage political dialogue which led to peace talks in Northern Ireland.
- During the darkest days of the "Troubles" he hosted peace talks in his plush Belfast home, where he invited key political and religious leaders and encourage a dialogue. This dialogue helped in ending 30 years' of terrorism. This was perhaps the most turbulent period in recent Irish history.
- He was appointed by Government of India as Honorary Consul for India to Northern Ireland from 2004-2012 and then reappointed in 2014 and continues till date.
- In March 2003 he was invited to the Buckingham Palace to have Lunch with her Majesty Queen Elizabeth II, of England, and Prince Philip Duke of Edinburgh.
- He was awarded the Most Excellent Order of the British Empire (MBE) in 1996.
- He was elected President of GOPIO (Global Organisation of People of Indian Origin) International in 2009 and is currently the Chairman of GOPIO International, headquartered in Mauritius.
- He is the first ethnic businessman to be elected President of the Northern Ireland Chamber of Commerce, the region's biggest business organisation.
- He has actively promoted business, education, political and cultural links between India and Northern Ireland, leading a series of business missions from Northern Ireland to India. Due to his efforts, India is the second biggest investor in Northern Ireland next to USA. Many Northern Ireland companies have set up businesses in India and vice versa.
- He holds honorary degrees from the region's two universities, Queen's University Belfast and the Ulster University, as well as from the Bengal Engineering and Science University.
- He was awarded Pravasi Bharti Samman Award by Dr Abdul Kalam, then President of India, in 2007 for his work in promoting links between U.K. and India, and outstanding service in peace efforts and charitable causes.
- He also holds awards for enterprise from the Confederation of British Industry in the UK and from the Northern Ireland Tourist Board for his work to promote tourism.
- He has been given various awards in recognition of his work in economic regeneration of Belfast, peace efforts, towards business and for developing educational and cultural links between Northern Ireland and India. He is one of the top N.R.I philanthropists in the United Kingdom.

At a time when business investors were afraid to invest in Belfast because of the terrorist attacks, Lord Rana developed a range of commercial properties for offices, shops and restaurants. This confidence in the future of Belfast particularly in the eighties was crucially important in reviving business activity and economic regeneration in the city and he still continues to do so.

He was the driving force in what became known as 'The Golden Mile', the entertainment heart of Belfast. He was also instrumental in the development of 'Harmony', an iconic statue of peace and reconciliation which is at the core of the city's Thanks giving Square.

He is the founder of Sanghol Education Complex which is funded by his foundation charitable trust in the UK. The institution provides university level education in disciplines such as Humanities, ICT, Business Management and Hotel and Hospitality Management, Teacher Training and Hair & Beauty vocational skills training. The Complex also includes an Indian Heritage Institute and has 2500 students studying there.

An Institute of Conflict Studies and Resolution Strategies is being planned to open shortly. The education complex is being developed to be approved and recognized as a private sector university by the government of Punjab.

ETHICS, GOVERNANCE AND CORPORATE SOCIAL RESPONSIBILITY IN INDIA

Issues and Perspectives

Editors
Professor Thomas G. Fraser
Dr Monika Aggarwal

KALPAZ

ISBN: 978-93-5128-195-5
Price: ₹ 850/-

First Published 2016

Published by

Kalpaz Publications
C-30, Satyawati Nagar,
Delhi - 110052
E-mail: kalpaz@hotmail.com Ph.: 9212142040

Printed at : G. Print Process, Delhi

Cataloging in Publication Data--DK

Courtesy: D.K. Agencies (P) Ltd. <docinfo@dkagencies.com>

International Conference on 'Business Ethics and Corporate Social Responsibility' (2013 : Sanghol, India)

Ethics, governance and corporate social responsibility in India : issues and perspectives / editors, Professor Thomas G. Fraser, Dr Monika Aggarwal.

pages cm

International Conference on 'Business Ethics and Corporate Social Responsibility' at Sanghol in November 2013.

ISBN 9789351281955

1. Business ethics--India--Congresses. 2. Social responsibility of business--India--Congresses. I. Fraser, T. G., editor. II. Aggarwal, Monika, 1975- editor. III. Title.

HF5387.5.I4I58 2013 DDC 174.40954 23

Contents

Foreword

Lord Diljit Rana

The Indian economy is passing through momentous times, with the country fast becoming one of the most dynamic in the world. Of course, history teaches us that progress brings challenges as well as opportunities and it is with that thought in mind that we hosted an International Conference on 'Business Ethics and Corporate Social Responsibility' at Sanghol in November 2013. The Conference also included a Memorial Lecture honouring the memory of that great patriot Lala Lajpat Rai who knew the critical importance of education. It was gratifying to see how many scholars were engaging with these important issues and this book brings many of their insights and reflections into the wider public forum.

The Lord Rana Edu City funded by the Lord Rana Foundation Charitable Trust, combines an educational institution and a village regeneration project at Sanghol, Punjab. The complex houses a group of degree awarding institutes specialising in the Humanities, Business Management, Teacher Training, Vocational Skills Training, Computer Sciences and Hospitality Management. It is also developing an Institute of Conflict Studies. In addition, there is a Higher Secondary School within the complex funded by the Foundation. In total, 2,500 students study at the Lord Rana Edu City, providing new opportunities for the people of this part of rural Punjab.

The complex was inaugurated by the late Dr Abdul Kalam in August 2006 when he was President of India. Its mission is in line with Dr Kalam's PURA concept of bringing quality education to rural communities. It also emphasis a conviction that education is a key means of tackling poverty.

Among the many unique aspects of the investment at Sanghol is the provision of education to children of construction workers and other poor parents' children at no cost. This reflects the overall commitment to promote quality education for all in this historic Punjab region.

The role of the complex extends beyond education being designed to raise social and medical conditions and offer greater economic opportunities. Health camps are conducted covering approximately 20,000 people from Sanghol and surrounding villages. People are checked for blood pressure, diabetes, vision, coronary scan and other conditions.

The complex is being developed to be an agent of economic regeneration and will include renewable energy projects such as solar technology. Economic development will also include agricultural and horticultural schemes. Another key initiative will see the area's history within the Indus Civilisation harnessed as a tourist attraction of significance (this will include the development of tourism in the area and provide opportunities for training to the Institute's hospitality management students and tourist guides). In this way Sanghol's dynamic future will be grounded on its rich heritage, a mirror of the country as a whole.

I am grateful to all those who so freely shared their expertise and insights.

Lord Rana MBE
Member House of Lords (British Parliament)
Founder & Funder
Lord Rana Edu City
Sanghol (Pb)

Preface

I wish to congratulate the editors, Professor Thomas G. Fraser and Dr Monika Aggarwal for their contributions in the editing and publishing of this book titled 'Ethics, Governance and Corporate Social Responsibility in India: Issues and Perspectives'. This ambitious goal was set for one purpose: to provide readers with the most comprehensive and current information covering the broad fields on the importance of CSR in a company.

In this edition the authors have aimed to find productive, knowledgeable and integrated information on the current CSR programmes prevalent in India and also on the formation of new policies, strategies and goals for creation of new CSR initiatives.

As my commitment to bring third level education and skills training to children in rural areas my charitable trust has funded this major educational and skills training centre at Sanghol, Punjab (www.cordia.edu.in) where the CSR conference on which this book is based was held in November 2013. The education project was inaugurated by Late Hon Abdul Kalam Ji in Aug 2006, then President of India. It is a not for profit initiative operated by my charitable trust. The education complex has about 2500 students of all age groups from school level to offering 18 graduate and post graduate courses in different streams.

I am committed to help promote educational and employment opportunities in rural areas such as this one by encouraging entrepreneurship. There is a great emphasis at the Campus for teaching entrepreneurial skills and encouraging innovative ideas.

70% of India's population lives in villages. Anybody who acquires a good job or moves up the economic ladder usually leaves the village and moves into the city, hence we are left rural population which is mostly poor, very poor or extremely poor. The future development of India is dependent on providing good quality education and skills training to the young. We live in a global world. We must educate, and arm our youth with proper skills to compete in the global market. The education project at Sanghol is an effort towards this objective. Our goal is to help people get out of poverty trap by bringing good education and skills training within their reach. The Late Shri Abdul Kalam Ji had coined a phrase "PURA", i.e. Providing Urban Facilities in Rural Areas. We have adopted this objective and we are working not only to improve facilities in village Sanghol but all the neighbouring villages to improve the quality of life in this area. I would urge the business leaders in India to focus on improving facilities in rural areas. They could adopt one or two villages. If villages do well, businesses will do well and India will become a powerful nation in every respect.

Even though I have been living outside India for nearly 55 years, but I am totally committed to serving India particularly investing time and effort to improve opportunities for the people living in this rural area of Punjab.

I hope that this book will provide great insights into the world of CSR and prove to be a valuable reference for researchers, policy experts and business professionals.

Lord Rana MBE
Member House of Lords (British Parliament)
Founder & Funder
Lord Rana Edu City
Sanghol (Pb)

Special Communication
Business Ethics and Corporate Social Responsibility

Urmil Verma

Ethics also known as "Moral Standards" or a "System of moral principles/values" examine ethical principles and problems that arise in a business environment. Business ethics are applicable in all spheres of business management and are relevant to the business conduct of individuals and the entire establishment. Ethics, not like the colour of skin, an individual inherits from his parents. It is the moral philosophy that involves basic principles of decent human conduct and the concepts of right and wrong behaviour. Business ethical norms reflect the norms of each historical period, which evolve with the passage of time.

Business Ethics is a term used very broadly throughout the world. Ethics of business is, whatever moral values and beliefs, individuals bring to the business activities. "Religion" is the most important factor in a person's perspective of business ethics with different opinions in different religions. Buddhists follow the teachings of Buddha to help with their ethics in business. Christianity uses the Ten Commandments and the teachings of Jesus Christ to clarify their ethics. The Jews use the Torah, while Muslims use the Quran and the teachings of the Prophet Muhammad to explain their views on business ethics. The basis of Hindu Ethics is "There is one all-prevailing Atman". It is the innermost soul of all beings.

In today's scenario, with the rapid pace of globalisation, it has become a must for organisations operating all over the world to adopt ethics in business. The twenty first century is characterised by unprecedented challenges and opportunities arising from the globalisation and the drive for inclusive development and the imperatives of climate change, global warming and global population. Indian business which is viewed globally as a responsible component of the predominance of India is poised now to take a leadership role. Indian entrepreneurs and business enterprise have a long tradition of working with the values that have defined our Nation's character for millennia.

India's ancient wisdom, which is very pertinent, guides people to think and work for the main objective of the well-being of the stakeholders including customers, employees, shareholders, management, community, society etc. The onus of business towards society is termed as Corporate Social Responsibility (CSR) which are categorised as economical, ethical, legal and philanthropic.

CSR is a concept which states that companies should not only consider their profits but also takes care of the interest of the society and the environment in which it operates. One of the most contemporary definitions is from the World Bank Group, stating "Corporate Social Responsibility is the commitment of business to contribute to sustainable economic development by working with employees, their families, local community and society at large to improve their lives in such ways that are good for business and for the development."

Every business house has an obligation to society; the philosophy is to give back to the society what it has taken from it, in the course of its quest for profit maximisation and wealth creation. Many of the business organisations have started recognising this fact. As Jack Ma, Founder and Executive Chairman of Alibaba Group. Alibaba-the Chinese e-commerce giant- gained international prominence after its recent record breaking IPO, has rightly pointed out in one of the very interesting blogs on business ethics—"When you have $1 million, you are a lucky person. When you have $10 million, you have trouble. When you have more than $1 billion, you have responsibility."

Ma says he has earmarked $3 billion of his IPO earnings to donate to environmental and educational projects in China. CEOs like Ma believe in giving back. On the corporate side, under his leadership Alibaba has pledged to donate 0.3 per cent of profits to environmental protection initiatives. There are numerous examples like this. As opined by Dr MacDonald, "If 0.3 per cent seems like a small amount, consider that that's a percentage of revenue, not profits. And on annual revenues in the $7.5 billion range, 0.3 per cent turns out to be a little over $22 million".

The CSR activities of Indian Business Houses are gradually increasing with the passage of time. There has been a long history of CSR in India and the Tata, being the pioneer, have been the role model on this path. About thousands of villages around Jamshedpur and Odisha are benefitted from development programmes run by the Tata Steel Rural Development Society. The Wipro has done a lot of work in two major areas i.e. education and natural disaster rehabilitation. Reliance Industries Ltd. has supported society through various projects in education and environment. CSR in Hindustan Lever Ltd. is rooted in its corporate purpose—the belief that "to succeed requires the highest standards of corporate behaviour towards our employees, consumers and the societies and world in which we live." Many other Indian

Business Houses like Godrej, Mahindra and Mahindra, Birla Group of Companies, Bajaj, Janki Devi Bajaj Gram Vikas Sanstha have taken up corporate social responsibilities to bring inclusive development in society.

Another amazing example of CSR activity is that of Andras House Ltd., from Belfast, Northern Ireland, UK established under the Chairmanship of Lord Diljit Rana. Andras House recognises education as one of the building blocks of any Nation and consider it as a priority area for its CSR activities with an aim to nurture young minds and educate them so that they contribute to the Nation's development. Realising the importance and relevance of education, an initiative to establish Cordia Group of Institutes was taken in 2006 to bring about a positive change in the lives of people living in Village Sanghol and also to the other states of the Nation though the instrument of Education. The CSR objective of company aims at "Investing in People" through medium of Education to transform their lives. From this endeavour in every academic year approximately 60 per cent girls of the total strength graduate in various disciplines who play great role in further improving the lives of so many families.

In brief, Corporate Social Responsibility is a vital element for any business corporations. There are many different areas in which a company may choose to focus its Corporate Social Responsibility like environment, education, health, nutrition and employment etc. India represents a very interesting case for understanding modern business ethics. India has been a land of Buddha, Chanakya, Ramakrishna and many other great souls and spirituals. The ethical environment of business in India is influenced by a variety of aspects of Indian history, norms, ideals and values. We reach the conclusion that Corporate Social Responsibility and maintenance of high ethical standards is not an option but is mandatory for all businesses.

We are extremely grateful to the Chief Editor Professor Thomas G. Fraser for his efforts and sincere dedication in compilation of the significant writings of the International Conference on Business Ethics and Corporate Social Responsibility organised in Cordia Group of Institutes in November 2013. We hope that researchers, academicians, policy-makers, professionals and society will benefit from the findings in this Compendium.

Introduction and Acknowledgements

Corporate Social Responsibility (CSR) is a management concept whereby companies integrate social and environmental concerns in their business operations and interactions with their stakeholders. CSR is generally understood as being the way through which a company achieves a balance of economic, environmental and social imperatives, while at the same time addressing the expectations of shareholders and stakeholders. Any business unit that implements a CSR concept, can bring along a variety of competitive advantages, such as enhanced access to capital and markets, increased sales and profits, operational cost savings, improved productivity and quality, efficient human resource base, improved brand image and reputation, enhanced customer loyalty, better decision-making and risk management processes.

The opening chapter of the book is dedicated to the Lala Lajpat Rai Memorial Lecture on "Lala Lajpat Rai and the pursuit of national education" delivered by Professor Thomas G. Fraser. This chapter brings to us Lala Ji's involvement, endeavour and contribution in the education sector in India. Lajpat Rai was a classic example of how someone could rise from comparatively humble origins in the rural Punjab to the commanding heights of the national movement through the power of education.

The second section of the book is devoted to the Business Ethics. Touching the issues like Gender Discrimination and Business Ethics in Indian Industry, Professor Shivani and Professor Ritu opined that in this modern world where we talk about equal rights for men and women, there are still some instances of people being discriminated because of their gender. Gender discrimination is an ethical problem and is not an issue which anyone can ignore or bear silently. It is considered as a serious form of injustice and is illegal in certain circumstances in most of the countries around the world. This paper covers various forms of gender discrimination, wage differentiation, occupational segregation, laws against gender discrimination and ways to promote gender equality in the workplace. The authors suggest that top management must avoid discriminatory practices in hiring, promotion, and facilities to the employees irrespective of what is his/her gender. The human resource managers should be careful while hiring and the promotion of the employees and providing facilities to employees in order to avoid any gender discrimination because it has a direct relationship on employee productivity. Discussing "Ancient Wisdom and Business Ethics", Dr Vaneeta and Dr Kusum tries to find out the origin of business ethics and its relationship with ancient wisdom. One may say that Jesus Christ was crucified even after being righteous but the real fact is that his teachings and lessons are being followed even today and he is worshipped by so many people. At the end of the millennium, we are back to basics. The study also expressed the views of various economists regarding the relationship between business and ethics. This resulted in three different views: Unitarian view, Separatist view and Integration view. This paper also discusses the need or necessity for business ethics - business in order to survive in the long run should concentrate on the welfare of society. Further, Professor Rashmi Kamra and Professor Gaurav Vij attempts to establish the relevance of ancient wisdom for innovative solutions to the mounting problems of business ethics. In pursuit of finding more sustainable management paradigms, there is a need to integrate the existing management model with ethical values in the ancient times through the spirituality wisdoms of the Vedas, Upanishads (Vedanta), Bhagavad Gita, Patanjali, Yoga aphorisms and Arthashashtra etc. to promote a more ethical and responsible leadership on an individual or institutional level.

The next section of the book covers the role of the stakeholders in building ethical society. Dr Sheojee Singh in his research on "Dream of an Ethical Society and the Dilemma of Capitalism" states that the present phase of human civilisation is beset with multiple transitional stages and the dilemma of ethics is one of such essential challenges of the present phase of life. The author attempts to analyse this prominent dilemma of our time in a logical and scientific way thereby providing a deeper insight into this and other related issues which adversely affect our happiness-index in day to day living. The author stresses on the fact that the dream of ethical society has been very dear to human imagination since time immemorial and it became a social necessity with the onward march of civilisation, but the conflicting demands put on the individual from various quarters of the immediate environment create a whirlpool of choices in action. Professor Renu Kalra in "Faith and Spirituality in an Increasingly Global Business Environment" struggles to find the exact meaning of spirituality. The author suggests that the organisations which are interested in exploring the advantages of workplace spirituality need to start at the beginning with a genuine commitment. The impact on spirituality in management is not automatic. It is a process that can take place, requiring efforts and vigilance. Dr Simranjit Kaur and Professor Monika Sharma examines the unethical behaviours, their causes, and the strategies for reducing their occurrence. The authors identify the causes of these unethical behaviours in organisations i.e. weak levels of supervision and accountability, inadequate administrative structure, lack of awareness of the public and employees, and unmonitored declaration of employee assets. Strategies to reduce the unethical behaviours include establishments of codes of business conduct and a whistle-blowing mechanism and a commitment by management to annual business ethics training for employees.

Professor Inderjeet Kaur attempted to identify the causes behind the economic crises that brought about dramatic consequences for the world economy and society. It exemplifies how CSR is subordinate to objectives of economic efficiency, in contrast to statements of companies which need to show adherence to responsible involvement in society. During the crisis, especially, CSR is viewed through the lens of its ability to promote company image and too little in terms of the link between business objectives and needs of society.

Education is a tool for total human development and if any one aspect of human personality is ignored, it can result very adversely. Professor Taruna and Professor Nidhi studied the relevance and role of professional ethics in teaching. The authors emphasised that the teachers should be concerned about the total improvement of students, which includes their intellectual level, understanding abilities, awareness of responsibilities, regard for elders, appreciation for cultural heritage and responsibility towards their fellow classmates. However, these above qualities are not seen in the present education system due to various changes such as modernisation, industrialisation, urbanisation, privatisation, globalisation as well the influence of western culture accompanied by many other problems and evils in Indian society that cause declining ethical values in Indian education system.

Very interesting segment of this edited book talks about environmental issues. It examines the linkage between tourism and Corporate Social Responsibility. The principles of sustainable tourism have been adopted by the tourism industry worldwide. Indian tourism sector is based on its unique endowments of biodiversity, forests, rivers, and its rich culture and heritage. The challenges in this sector lie in successfully preserving these in their original form, and making them accessible to domestic and international travellers, together with safeguarding the economic interest and heritage of local communities. In his empirical research on "Plausible Linkage between and Sustainable Tourism: A Qualitative Study of Tourism Business Units in Himachal Pradesh", Professor Arun Sharma aimed at examining the linkage between CSR and sustainable tourism. He found that the present scenario is an alarming stage for whole world to care for the resources available on earth. This is only possible if everybody will understand his/ her own responsibility and become equally responsible for every business practice. More and more firms are registering everyday for manufacturing and distributing the new products and services, the businessmen hardly bothers about their CSR - corporate social responsibility. Dr Anurag Sankhian talked about "Adopting sustainable and eco-friendly mechanisms of human development" and suggests that this is necessary for saving the natural beauty of the Himalayan valleys. He opined that the ongoing construction of the Neogal Hydro power projects are creating lots of environmental challenges along with ongoing conflict between the construction companies, local administration and various state government departments related with the problems. There is a need to protect and conserve Neogal River to ensure clean and sustainable development of the Palampur valley. The major problems associated with the construction of the power project in the valley include, environmental degradation, large scale deforestation, adverse health impacts on residents near project site, blockage of Irrigation Channels, Impact on Drinking water quality and Supply, and Muck dumping in forest areas. Professor Amit Katoch and Dr Prashant Gautam inspects the rural tourism resources of the villages around Dharamshala. The authors further focuses on identifying the rural population's understanding of rural tourism's development and its consequent benefits. Further, the research examines the willingness of the communities to participate in rural tourism. Professor Amit Kashyap and Professor Shashi Bala Kashyap attempt to combine law and science for environment protection and management which provides a new global perspective, a new paradigm. It may provide a new structure for a scientific revolution with emphasis on the biologist view of the world and the natural systems. Ecology and international law provide a new mechanism to shape global environments. This combination is likely to evolve sustainable development. Above all, it will help adaptation of human beings to different ecological systems including different cultures.

We are deeply beholden to the eminent researchers and scholars from different universities and colleges who have contributed their valuable research papers and articles to enable us to bring this compilation.

We feel indebted to The Rt. Hon. The Lord Rana, MBE, Baron of Malone, Chairman, Lord Rana Foundation Charitable Trust, UK for his continuous encouragement and support.

We express our sincere gratitude to Ms Urmil Verma, Director, Lord Rana Foundation Charitable Trust, and Executive Trustee, Smt Jawala Devi Memorial Trust, India, who remained a source of inspiration and motivated us to undertake this project.

We appreciate and are thankful to the Kalpaz Publication for publishing this project.

Last but not the least we would like to deeply thank all those who provided us all sort of support and assistance during several months in which this endeavour lasted.

'Any views expressed in this book are those of the authors of the chapters and do not necessarily represent those of the editors, the Lord Rana Edu City, the Lord Rana Foundation Charitable Trust, UK, or the Smt Jawala Devi Memorial Trust, India'.

Professor Thomas G. Fraser
Dr Monika Aggarwal

List of Contributors

Amit Kashyap, Sr. Research Fellow, Department of Laws, H.P. University, Shimla.

Amit Katoch, Research Scholar (Tourism), Central University of Himachal Pradesh, Dharamshala, Kangra, Himachal Pradesh.

Anurag Sankhian, Assistant Professor (Geography), Government College of Education Sector 20 D, Chandigarh.

Arun Sharma, Research Scholar, Tourism Management. Dept. of Tourism STTHM, Central University of Himachal Pradesh, Dharmshala TAB-Shahpur.

Gaurav Vij, Assistant Professor in Commerce, D.A.V College, Abohar.

Harish Kumari, Principal, Khalsa College (Amritsar) of Technology and Business Studies, Mohali.

Inderjeet Kaur, Researcher. Guru Nanak Dev University, Amritsar.

Kusum Gupta, Assistant Professor in Commerce, D.A.V. College, Bathinda.

Manmeet Kaur, Lecturer, Guru Nanak Khalsa College for Women, Gujarkhan Campus, Model Town, Ludhiana.

Monika Sharma, Assistant Professor, Cordia Institute of Business Management, Sanghol.

Nidhi Palta, Assistant Professor, Smt. Jawala Devi College of Education, Sanghol.

Prashant Kumar Gautam, Assistant Professor (Tourism), University Institute of Hotel Management and Tourism (UIHMT), Panjab University, Chandigarh.

Professor Thomas G. Fraser

Punpreet Kaur, Lecturer, Guru Nanak Khalsa College for Women, Gujarkhan Campus, Model Town, Ludhiana.

Rakhi J. Singh, Dev Samaj College for Women, Sector 45-B, Chandigarh.

Rashmi Kamra, Assistant Professor in Commerce, D.A.V. College, Abohar.

Renu Kalra, Dev Samaj College for Women, Sector 45-B, Chandigarh.

Ritu Kalra, Assistant Professor, Deptt. of Commerce and Business Management, DAV College, Abohar.

Shashi Bala Kashyap, Assistant Professor, Botany Department, SCD Govt. College, Ludhiana.

Sheojee Singh, Senior Asst. Professor C.E.S.(I), Govt. College of Education, Chandigarh.

Shivani Setia, Assistant Professor, Deptt. of Commerce and Business Management, DAV College, Abohar.

Simranjit Kaur, Head of Department, Cordia Institute of Business Management, Sanghol.

Taruna Narang, Assistant Professor, Smt. Jawala Devi College of Education, Sanghol.

Urmil Verma, Director, Lord Rana Foundation Charitable Trust, UK, and Executive Trustee, Smt Jawala Devi Memorial Trust, India.

Vaneeta Rani, Associate Professor in Commerce, Government Bikram College of Commerce, Patiala.

1

Lala Lajpat Rai and the Pursuit of National Education

Lala Lajpat Rai Memorial Lecture

Professor Thomas G. Fraser

Lala Lajpat Rai, whose death on 17 November 1928 this lecture commemorates, was neither an educator nor an educationalist in the accepted sense of these terms. Never a university or college professor, nor a schoolmaster, nevertheless a concern for education, especially national education, runs as a consistent thread through his life and career. The period of the late nineteenth and early twentieth centuries was a time of great intellectual ferment in India as educated men and women like him explored the possibilities and implications of national independence. The men who formed the nascent Indian National Congress in 1885 were overwhelmingly the products of an educational system primed by Thomas Babington Macaulay's Minute on Education of 1835, and rather too readily put into effect by the Governor-General, Lord William Bentinck. Few documents in modern Indian history have been the subject of more analysis, and criticism, than this, setting in place as it did an educational policy based upon the English language and principles then in vogue in the West. The thrust of the Minute was the creation of an educated elite which would act as an intermediary between rulers and ruled and which would by implication at least help sustain the fabric of British rule. As an instrument of imperial policy it proved to be a two edged sword, since it succeeded in setting in place a local elite of administrators, teachers and lawyers, but it was also part of the process which encouraged these very people to argue that Indians should rule themselves, not least since the higher rungs of the administration were in practice the preserve of British personnel.

From the perspective of the twenty first century it is easy to criticise Macaulay and Bentinck for their dismissal of established Indian learning, but they were men of their time and it was a time when western concepts and techniques were in the ascendant. The type of education they set in hand ignored the indigenous educational systems which had long served the Hindus and Muslims. In the former, Sanskrit based learning was imparted by *gurus* to their *chelas*, while in the latter Islamic teaching was imparted by scholarly instructors, generally attached to a mosque. In each case, the teacher was a highly respected member of society. The western educational principles set out in what might be called the Macaulay-Bentinck system of education have been criticised as contributing to the undermining of traditional Indian society under imperial rule.[1]

Some of the shortcomings of the new policy were addressed in the East India Company's education despatch of 1854, which led to the establishment of universities in the presidency cities of Calcutta, Bombay and Madras and put in place a scheme of grant-in-aid to encourage the creation of local schools where instruction of a practical nature would be in the local languages[2]. The system was open to several criticisms, perhaps the most pertinent of which were that at the higher levels its base was urban, barely touching in practice the rural communities which formed some 80 per cent of the population, and that it drew a line between between those educated through local languages and the elite who were able to attend the English language institutions. Progress at the local level was uneven, but by 1882, when Lajpat Rai was a pupil at just such a local school, there were some 90,000 schools teaching 2.25 million pupils[3]. Even so, when independence came in 1947 the country's literacy rate had not passed 20 per cent. The only sense in which the Indian educational system of the late nineteenth century could be described as 'national' was that through the medium of the English language it provided an ease of communication for people from across the country just as Persian had done for many in the areas which had been under Mughal control and influence.

Lajpat Rai was a classic example of how someone could rise from comparatively humble origins in the rural Punjab to the commanding heights of the national movement through the power of education. He came of a family for whom education was of the essence. His father, Radha Kishan, came of that first generation of teachers trained in the 1860s as a result of the new policies established in the 1854 despatch. In his summative work, *The Problem of National Education in India,* which was serialised in 1919 and then published as a book in 1920, Lajpat Rai paid a heartfelt tribute to his father, to whom he ascribed his interest in education and whose gifts as a teacher he clearly recollected with gratitude and affection, founding a school in his memory in his home town[4]. Radha Kishan was determined that his son should get the best possible education, beyond the opportunities available to him in the small town of Jagraon near Ludhiana where they lived. The young Lajpat Rai, who did not enjoy robust health, followed his education briefly in Delhi and then on a scholarship at the Mission High School at Ludhiana. His success enabled him to qualify in law at Lahore University College, a government institution then still under the authority of Calcutta University.[5]

During his time in Lahore, at the invitation of Lala Madhan Singh and Lala Sain Das, in December 1882 he joined the Arya Samaj, the movement which had been founded in 1875 by Swami Dayanand Saraswati. The Arya Samaj had a powerful appeal for idealistic young Hindus and three years after its founder's death in 1883 the Dayanand Anglo-Vedic (DAV) School was established in the city. Lajpat Rai was associated from the start with the new venture, which became the Dayanand Anglo-Vedic College in 1889. The DAV College proved to be a pioneer in the pursuit of education in the Punjab, being followed in 1892 by the Muslims' Islamia College at Lahore and then by the establishment of the Sikh Khalsa College at Amritsar in 1897.[6] Nationally, the DAV College was not first in the field, since in 1875 the Mohammedan Anglo-Oriental College had been founded at Aligarh in the United Provinces. In 1885, the Deccan Education Society, in which the leading Maharashtrian figures Bal Gangadhar Tilak and Gopal Ganesh Agarkar were to the fore, established the Fergusson College at Poona, named after the Governor of the Bombay Presidency, Sir James Fergusson[7]. Then, in 1898 the Central Hindu College, later the Benares Hindu University, was established at Benares.

When it opened in June 1889 the DAV College enrolled around a dozen students, but from this modest beginning by 1913 that number had grown to 903, with 1737 in the associated School. The guiding hand behind the School and College from their inception was a young graduate, Lala Hans Raj, who served them throughout their difficult early years. The basic principle followed was a kind of synthesis of traditional values together with an acknowledgement that India needed to learn from the current scientific and technological predominance of the West. Sanskrit was to be studied alongside western literature. Two things set the DAV College apart from the government institutions; namely, that the teaching staff was exclusively Indian and that the venture was entirely self-financed, the latter no easy challenge[8]. One of the youthful Lajpat Rai's first public interventions came on 3rd March 1884 when he appealed to wealthy supporters to help with the proposed educational venture, noting the lack of progress thus far.[9]

Involved in the project since its inception, from 1891 he was closely involved in the College's Managing Committee, becoming its honorary secretary. But education was only one of his many activities. Not content with pursuing a successful legal career, he was a leading figure behind the formation of the Punjab National Bank. He also became something of an author, publishing between 1896 and 1900 under the general title 'Great Men of the World', biographies of the Italian patriots Giuseppe Mazzini and Giuseppe Garibaldi, as well of Shivaji, Swami Dayanand and Shri Krishna. In the case of the first two there was the thinly disguised parallel between Italy under Austrian and French domination and the situation of India at the turn of the century. In his preface to the Mazzini volume, Lajpat Rai addressed the issue of education, arguing that a country could only gain its independence when it had reached the same educational level as the country ruling it.[10] As early as 1888, he had been active in the Indian National Congress, his political profile achieving national status in 1907 when he was deported to Mandalay in Burma as a result of his support for agrarian protests in Punjab. Along with the Bengali Bipin Chandra Pal and Tilak, he became part of the celebrated political trio 'Lal, Bal, Pal'. It was as a result of his increasing political prominence that in 1910 he resigned from the College's governing body, not wishing it to attract government disapproval.[11]

His views had already set off alarm bells in official circles. That this had happened was in part at least the result of a speech on education which he delivered at the end of 1905. Much of that year had been spent travelling in Britain, Europe and the United States, where he made it his business to observe their educational systems and think about their lessons for India. These were explored in a speech to the Arya Samaj on 26 November 1905 and which he subsequently published. Entitled a 'Call to the Youth to Make Sacrifices for the Progress of the Nation', the speech embodied much of what he had seen in Europe. Posing the question of why Europe was supreme in the world, he focussed upon the Europeans' capacity for organisation, the secret behind this being the system of education. His depiction of European, especially British, education was overly rosy, but he was seeking to pinpoint aspects which could be applied at home. Among the features which had impressed him was compulsory education for both sexes. A nation could not be great, he argued, unless its mothers were great. He pointed to the provision of books and pens and that needy children were given food in France and by London County Council. The system of night schools opened up possibilities for higher education for people of modest backgrounds, and he noted that such schools in London had better apparatus than the best Indian educational institutions. He also stressed the importance given to physical education compared with India. His attention then turned to factories in Punjab, which he claimed were not progressing owing to lack of the necessary skills. All of these observations had led him to the conclusion that the only way that they could protect themselves from the advance of western civilisation was to adopt its methods. His conclusion was more overtly political, appealing to the youth of Punjab for self-sacrifice, the national tree requiring the blood of martyrs. It was this latter sentiment which the government used against him in 1907.[12]

Despite severing his formal link with the running of the DAV College in 1910, he had no intention of abandoning his interest in educational work. He had continued to visit Britain and in April 1914 left for London as part of an Indian National Congress delegation, which included his fellow lawyers, Bhupendra Nath Basu from Bengal and M.A. Jinnah from Bombay. It proved to be a long exile. He was still in the country when Britain went to war with Germany on 4th August 1914. In November, he left for the United States. Like most of his contemporaries he probably expected a short conflict, but the reality proved to be tragically different and he was not able to return to India until February 1920. During this period he travelled extensively in the United States, and also took the opportunity to visit Japan, whose educational system he had previously studied at second hand.

A consistent theme running through Lajpat Rai's educational writings is his intellectual curiosity about what was being practised in other countries. His time in the United States was put to good effect in the publication of two studies. In *England's Debt to India: A Historical Narrative of Britain's Fiscal Policy in India* he castigated, amongst other things, Britain's educational record in the country. Quoting official figures for 1912, he said that of the total population of 315,156,386, the school enrolment was 6,781,000, from which he calculated that 82 per cent of boys and 95 per cent of girls were receiving no schooling. He criticised both the length of time spent in education and the comparative lack of vocational training, which accounted for 12,064 pupils. In higher education there were 179 colleges affiliated to seven universities. Of the 36,533 students, 28,196 were in arts courses. By contrast, there were 3,046 law students, 1,822 in medical colleges, 1,607 in engineering colleges and a mere 267 studying agriculture, the work of the majority of people. The government, he concluded, had made no provision for the education of the mass of the population.[13]

This, then, brings us to his major treatise on the subject, *The Problem of National Education in India*, written while he was in the United States in 1918 and which appeared in book form in London in 1920. By then he had over three decades of close involvement in educational affairs, as well as extensive experience of Britain, the United States and Japan. In his book he quoted widely from American and British educational authorities, devoting an entire chapter to the policies of the President of the Board of Education, H.A.L. Fisher. In considering the context of the book it is important to remember the quickening pace of political life in India as a result of the war, with the conclusion of the Lucknow Pact, the formation of the Home Rule Leagues of Tilak and Annie Besant, and the genesis of what became the Montagu-Chelmsford reforms. Although it was published in

1920, the text was written before the tragic events of 1919 changed the political map of India for ever.

He started his treatise by reminding his readers of his long connection with the DAV College in Lahore. The College was, he claimed, more genuinely national than the institutions at Aligarh and Benares, since they had always had Europeans on their staff and had received government funds, while that at Poona was named after a foreigner. The DAV College had from the start only employed Indians. While expressing his respect for Sanskrit, he did not see it as the way forward, except for a few scholars. This was equally true of Arabic and Persian. If India were to progress, it had to be through the medium of modern languages, both Indian and foreign. The national language of India would be Hindustani, with Hindus and Muslims using their different scripts. Hindustani should be the basis of instruction, together with the appropriate provincial language, the use of what he termed local dialects being discouraged. In the second half of the elementary school English was to be compulsory, but not as a means of instruction. Children were to be taught the classic trio of reading, writing and arithmetic, as well as patriotism, hygiene, drawing, Indian geography and history, world geography, civics, music and modelling. Just as he had done in his speech to the Arya Samaj in 1905, he was appealing for a concept of national education which he believed would strengthen the nation by making it look to the future. National education had to be distinguished from local, provincial, denominational or sectarian education. Should Indians, he challenged his readers, ignore the modern sciences in medicine, surgery, hygiene, engineering, banking, commerce and insurance? It would be folly, he argued, to discourage the study of European languages, literature and sciences.[14]

From the time of his return to India in February 1920 until his death in 1928, Lajpat Rai was never far from the forefront of national politics. In September 1920 he presided over the special session of the Indian National Congress, and became a strong supporter of Gandhi's *satyagraha* campaign, twice being imprisoned. As a member of the

Swarajya Party, which had broken away from Congress under Motilal Nehru and C.R. Das, he was a prominent participant in the working of the Central Legislative Assembly which had been set up under the Montagu-Chelmsford reforms, subsequently with Madan Mohan Malaviya forming the Independent Congress Party. He continued to be a frequent visitor to Britain and travelled widely in Europe. None of this left him with much time for educational matters. His major initiative was the establishment of the Tilak School of Politics in Lahore in 1920, the work of which carried over into the Servants of the People Society, which remains a central part of his legacy for modern India.[15]

As one of the principal building blocks of the nation it was only right that Indian nationalist leaders should consider the future of education, especially since the system then in place had been imposed from outside. Lajpat Rai was not unique. His views, however, command respect. His engagement with education was keenly felt and deeply personal. Without ever compromising his sense of Indian identity or respect for traditional values, he sought out through travel and reading the best educational practices of his time. He was quite prepared to advocate and adapt western methods as a means of countering the imperial dominance the West then enjoyed. The creation and growth of the DAV educational movement, independent of the government sector, owed much to the commitment which he brought to it in its difficult early stages when the necessary finance was hard to come by. Anyone who has been associated with the growth of a new institution knows of the challenges which need to be faced and overcome. How he would have contributed to the subsequent debates on the shape of education in a free India can only be a matter of conjecture, but through his practical work and his extensive writings his legacy was firmly in place at the time of his untimely death.

References

1. Lachmann Dass Bhimbat, Editor, Randeep Wadehra, *Evolution of Education ill India. A historical perspective* (Chandigarh, Mrs Adarsh, 2012, Printed in Great Britain by Amazon.co.uk Ltd., Marston Gate), pp. 17-18.

2. R.J. Moore, *Sir Charles Wood's Indian Policy 1853-66* (Manchester, Manchester University Press: 1966), pp 109-23.
3. *The Imperial Gazetteer of India. The Indian Empire.* Vol. IV, *Administrative* (Oxford, The Clarendon Press: 1909), pp. 412-14.
4. *The Problem of National Education ill India,* serialized in 1919 and published as a book in 1920, B.R, Nanda, Chief Editor, *The Collected Works of Lala Lajpat Rai,* Volume Seven, Manohar Publishers and Distributors, New Delhi, 200S, Servants of the People Society, p. 131 (hereafter, Nanda, Chief Editor, *Collected Works).*
5. The story of my life', Nanda, Chief Editor, *Collected Works,* Volume Five, 2004, pp 286-8.
6. *Imperial Gazetteer of India.Provincial Series, Punjab,* Vol. I. Superintendent of Government Printing Calcutta, (reprinted Usha Publications, New Delhi, 1984) 1908, p. 136.
7. Ram Gopal, *Lokamanya Tilak,* London, Asia Publishing House: 19S6, Reprinted 1965, pp 3S~7.
8. ldeals of D.A. V. College and Responsibilities of its Alumni in England', Presidential speech at D.A.V. College foundation day dinner, London, IS June 1914, *The Tribune,* 7 August 1914, Nanda, Chief Editor, *Collected Works,* Volume Five, 2004, pp. 24-35.
9. Dayanand Anglo-Vedic College', 3 March 1884, Nanda, Chief Editor, *Collected Works,* Volume One, 2003, pp. 75-76.
10. Giuseppe Mazzini -A Biography, Lahore, 1896, Nanda, Chief Editor, *Collected Works,* Volume One, 2003, p. 290.
11. Ideals of D.A.V. College', Nanda, Chief Editor, *Collected Works,* Volume Five, 2004, p. 24.
12. A Call to the Youth to Make Sacrifices for Progress of the Nation', 26 November 1905, Nanda. Chief Editor, *Collected Works,* Volume Two, 2003, pp. 343-52
13. England's Debt to India: A Historical Narrative of Britain's Fiscal Policy in India, 1917, Nanda, Chief Editor, *Collected Works,* Volume Seven, 200S, pp. 352-57.
14. The Problem of National Education in India. Nanda, Chief Editor, *Collected Works,* Volume Seven, 200S, pp. 129-235.
15. The Tilak School of Politics', 7 and 21 March 1926, Nanda, Chief Editor, *Collected Works,* Volume Twelve, 2009, pp. 406-11.

2

Corporate Social Responsibilities and Business Ethics

Dr Harish Kumari

Introduction

A business enterprise should do business and earn money in ways that fulfill the expectations of the society. Every individual living in society has certain obligations towards society. He has to respect social values and norms of behaviour. A business enterprise is permitted by society to carry on industrial or commercial activities and thereby earn profits. But it is obligatory on the part of the business enterprise not to do anything, that is undesirable from society's point of view. Manufacture and sale of adulterated goods, making deceptive advertisements, not paying taxes which are due, polluting the environment and exploiting workers are some examples of socially undesirable practices which may increase the profit of enterprises but which have adverse effect on society at large. On the other hand, supplying good quality goods, creating healthy working conditions, honestly paying taxes prevention/installing pollution devices in the factory, and sincerely attending to customer complaints are examples of socially desirable practices which improve the image of enterprises and also make them profitable. In fact, it is through socially responsible and ethically upright behaviour that business enterprises can get durable success.

Concept of Corporate Social Responsibility

Social responsibility of business refers to its obligation to take those decisions and perform those actions which are desirable in terms of the objectives and values of our society. The assumption of social responsibilities by business enterprises implies that they respect the aspirations of society and would try their best to contribute to the achievement of these aspirations along with their profit interests. This idea is in contrast to the common notion that business exists only for maximising profits for its owners and it is irrelevant to talk of public good. It follows that a 'X' is a young newspaper reporter and has been writing for almost six months on malpractices by business enterprises including such issues as misleading advertisements, supply of adulterated products, poor working conditions, environmental pollution, bribing government officials, and so on. He has started believing that business people tend to do anything to mint money. He happens to take an interview of 'Y', chairman of a leading truck manufacturing company which is known for its fair dealing with customers, employees, investors as well as other social groups. Through this interview, 'X' develops the understanding that it is possible for a business enterprise to be socially responsible and ethically upright and, at the same time, be highly profitable. He then gets busy with studying more about the social responsibility of business and business ethics responsible business, and indeed any responsible member of society, must act with due concern for the effects on the lives of other people. In this sense, social responsibility is broader than legal responsibility of business. Legal responsibility may be fulfilled by mere compliance with the law. Social responsibility is more than that. It is a firm's recognition of social obligations even though not covered by law, along with the obligations laid down by law. In other words, social responsibility involves an element of voluntary action on the part of business people for the benefit of society.

Objective

The objective of this paper is to explain the concept of social responsibility, discuss the need for social responsibility and identify the social responsibility towards different interest groups.

Review of Literature

Enrico Cavalier in the study titled, "Ethics and Corporate Social Responsibility" has mentioned that the ethics we find in companies contains the same elements as the ethics in the socio-economic context in which they operate. The aspirations and ethical levels of companies operating in certain countries differ substantially from those of companies operating in other areas, where the defence of the environment, social welfare, human rights, cooperation, assistance are expected and offered to a lower degree, or are not requested or protected at all. The new globalised, networked economy, based on the coordinated management of knowledge, sets evolutionary trends in motion that raise the level of ethicality, but simultaneously generates a braking effect on the ethical contents of corporate behaviour. Luis and Javier in their paper titled, "Corporate Social Responsibility and Business Ethics: An Interpretative Proposal" has provided that corporate social responsibility poses a major challenge, as it represents a more complex way of administering and managing companies and organisations, from which new demands emerge: transparency, multi-stakeholder dialogue, Triple Bottom Line. It is further provided that corporate social responsibility is evidently a point of departure or rather a stop on route but not a destination; it is a way give the system a push to stimulate it to reach higher goals. Bhanu Murthy, in his study titled, "Business Ethics and Corporate Responsibility – A New Perspective" has concluded that there has a controversy over the need for business ethics. The controversy had a misplaced emphasis. Today it is most urgently felt that different dimensions, namely, social responsibility, environmental accountability and governance must be brought under one umbrella of business ethics. The top management must bring about organisational transformation so as to make such a trifocal approach sustainable. However, the major challenge is of evolving a strategy for laying down standards that take care of major issues and provide standards that are measurable, objective and universal. The three central issues of International Social Responsibility Standards are: 1. Acceptance of the tri-focal approach – Governance, Responsibility and Accountability. 2. Approach to methods of measurement is resolved. 3. The mandatory versus voluntary issue can be resolved only if issues of measurement and their universal applicability is resolved.

Social Responsibilities of Business and Business Ethics

There are different opinions regarding responsibility of business. Some considers that it is towards its owners only while others, however, hold an opposite view and argue that the firm has a social responsibility to serve all sections of society who are affected by its decisions and actions. It would be useful to understand the arguments offered both in favour of and against the assumption of social responsibilities by business.

Arguments for Social Responsibility

(i) *Justification for existence and growth:* Business exists for providing goods and services to satisfy human needs. Though, profit motive is an important justification for undertaking business activity, it should be looked upon as an outcome of service to the people. In fact, the prosperity and growth of business is possible only through continuous service to society. Thus, assumption of social responsibility by business provides justifications for its existence and growth.

(ii) *Long-term interest of the firm:* A firm and its image stand to gain maximum profits in the long run when it has its highest goal as 'service to society'. When increasing number of members of society — including workers, consumers, shareholders, government officials, feel that business enterprise is not serving its best interest, they will tend to withdraw their cooperation to the enterprise concerned. Therefore, it is in its own interest if a firm fulfills it's social responsibility. The public image of any firm would also be improved when it supports social goals.

(iii) *Avoidance of government regulation:* From the point of view of a business, government regulations are undesirable because they limit freedom. Therefore, it is believed that businessmen can avoid the problem of government regulations by voluntarily assuming social responsibilities, which helps to reduce the need for new laws.

(iv) *Maintenance of society:* The argument here is that laws cannot be passed for all possible circumstances. People who feel that they are not getting their due from the business may resort to anti-social activities, not necessarily governed by law. This may harm the interest of business itself. Therefore, it is desirable that business enterprises should assume social responsibilities.

(v) *Availability of resources with business:* This argument holds that business institutions have valuable financial and human resources which can be effectively used for solving problems. For example, business has a pool of managerial talent and capital resources, supported by years of experience in organising business activities. It can help society to tackle its problems better, given the huge financial and human resources at its disposal.

(vi) *Converting problems into opportunities:* Related with the preceding argument is the argument that business with its glorious history of converting risky situations into profitable deals, can not only solve social problems but it can also make them effectively useful by accepting the challenge.

(vii) *Better environment for doing business:* If business is to operate in a society which is full of diverse and complicated problems, it may have little chance of success. Therefore, it is argued that the business system should do something to meet needs before it is confronted with a situation when its own survival is endangered due to enormous social illnesses. A society with fewer problems provides better environment for a firm to conduct its business.

(viii) *Holding business responsible for social problems:* It is argued that some of the social problems have either been created or perpetuated by business enterprises themselves. Environmental pollution, unsafe workplaces, corruption in public institutions, and discriminatory practices in employment are some of these problems. Therefore, it is the moral obligation of business to get involved in solving these problems, instead of merely expecting that other social agencies will deal with them on their own.

Arguments against Social Responsibility

The major arguments against social responsibility are:

(i) *Violation of profit maximisation objective:* According to this argument, business exists only for profit maximisation. Therefore, any talk of social responsibility is against this objective. In fact, business can best fulfill its social responsibility if it maximises profits through increased efficiency and reduced costs.

(ii) *Burden on consumers:* It is argued that social responsibilities like pollution control and environmental protection are very costly and often require huge financial investments. In such circumstances, businessmen are likely to simply shift this burden of social responsibility by charging higher prices from the consumers instead of bearing it themselves. Therefore, it is unfair to tax the consumers in the name of social responsibility.

(iii) *Lack of social skills:* All social problems cannot be solved the way business problems are solved. In fact, businessmen do not have the necessary understanding and training to solve social problems. Therefore, according to this argument, social problems should be solved by other specialised agencies.

(iv) *Lack of broad public support:* Here the argument is that the public in general does not like business involvement or interference in social programmes. Therefore, business cannot operate successfully because of lack of public confidence and cooperation in solving social problems.

Social Responsibility towards Different Interest Groups

Once the social objective of business is recognised, it is important to know to whom and for what the business and its management are responsible. Obviously, a business unit has to decide in which areas it should carry out social goals. Some of the specific responsibilities and enterprise may be outlined as under:

(i) *Responsibility towards the shareholders or owners:* A business enterprise has the responsibility to provide a fair return to the shareholders or owners on their capital investment and to ensure the safety of such investment. The corporate enterprise on a company form of organisation must also provide the shareholders with regular, accurate and full information about its working as well as schemes of future growth.

(ii) *Responsibility towards the workers:* Management of an enterprise is also responsible for providing opportunities to the workers for meaningful work. It should try to create the right kind of working conditions so that it can win the cooperation of workers. The enterprise must respect the democratic rights of the workers to form unions. The worker must also be ensured of a fair wage and a fair deal from the management.

(iii) *Responsibility towards the consumers:* Supply of right quality and quantity of goods and services to consumers at reasonable prices constitutes the responsibility of an enterprise toward its customers. The enterprise must take proper precaution against adulteration, poor quality, lack of desired service and courtesy to customers, misleading and dishonest advertising, and so on. They must also have the right of information about the product, the company and other matters having a bearing on their purchasing decision.

(iv) *Responsibility towards the government and community:* An enterprise must respect the laws of the country and pay taxes regularly and honestly. It must behave as a good citizen and act according to the well accepted values of the society. It must protect the natural environment and should avoid bad, effluent, smoky chimneys, ugly buildings, dirty working conditions. It must also develop a proper image in society through continuous interaction with various groups of people.

Conclusion

Social responsibility of business refers to its obligation to take those decisions and perform those actions which are desirable in terms of the objectives and values of our society. Corporate social responsibility is required for justification of existence and growth, long-term interest of the firm, avoidance of government regulation, maintenance of society, availability of resources with business, Converting problems into opportunities, better environment for doing business and holding business responsible for social problems but in some cases it indirectly burdens consumers and also lacks broad public support. The specific responsibilities and enterprise had may been outlined towards shareholders or owners, a consumers, workers, government and community.

References

Adams, C. A. 2002. 'Internal Organisational Factors Influencing Corporate Social and Ethical Reporting: Beyond Current Theorising'. *Accounting, Auditing and Accountability Journal*, 15(2): 223–50.

Ahmed, Akbar, 'A Muslim Meditation on Love', beliefnet, 15th February, 2003.

Altes, Korthals, 'Ethical and Religious Perspectives on Social Development in the European Union', WCRP Symposium on Ethical and Religious Perspectives on Social Development. (9th March, 1995, Copenhagen.)

Alkhafaji, A. F. 1989. *A Stakeholder Approach to Corporate Governance: Managing in a Dynamic Environment*. New York: Quorum.

Anderson, J. C., and Frankle, A. W. 1980. 'Voluntary Social Reporting: An Iso-Beta Portfolio Analysis'. *The Accounting Review*, 55: 467–79.

Argyris, C., and Schon, D. A. 1978. Organisational Learning: A Theory of Action Perspective. Reading, Mass.: Addison-Wesley. Aupperle, K. E., Carrol, A. B., and Hatfield, J. D. 1985. 'An Empirical Examination of the Relationship between Corporate Social Responsibility and Profitability'. *Academy of Management Journal*, 28(2): 446–63.

Bansal, P., and Roth, K. 2000. 'Why Companies Go Green: A Model of Ecological Responsiveness'. *Academy of Management Journal*, 43: 717–36.

Barnett, M. L., and Salomon, R. M. 2003. 'Throwing a Curve at Socially Responsible Investing Research'. *Organisation and Environment*, 16(3): 381–9.

Barney, J. B. 1991. 'Firm Resources and Sustained Competitive Advantage'. Journal of Management, 17(1): 99–120. and Hansen, M. H. 1994. 'Trustworthiness as a Source of Competitive Advantage'. *Strategic Management Journal*, 15: 175–90.

Berger, P. L., and Luckmann, T. 1966. *The Social Construction of Reality: A Treatise in the Sociology of Knowledge*. Garden City, NY: Doubleday.

Berman, S. L., Wicks, A. C., Kotha, S., and Jones, T. M. 1999. 'Does Stakeholder Orientation Matter? The Relationship between Stakeholder Management Models and Firm Financial Performance'. *Academy of Management Journal*, 42(5): 488–506.

Bhattacharya, C. B., and Sen, S. 2004. 'Doing Better at Doing Good: When, Why, and How Consumers Respond to Corporate Social Initiatives'. *Californial Management Review*, 47(1): 9–24.

Gundlach, Gregory D. and Patrick E. Murphy (1993), "Ethical and Legal Foundations of Relational Marketing Exchanges," *Journal of Marketing*, 57 (October), 35-46

Klein S. (2000), "Drucker as Business Moralist", *Journal of Business Ethics*, Volume 28, Number 2, November, 121-128(8).

Klempner, Geoffrey (2006), "On being a Business Philosopher", *Philosophies for Business*. E-journal. Issue 26, 5 February.

Murthy, K.V.B. and R. Jha (2006), *Environmental Sustainability – A Consumption Approach*, Routledge, London and New York.

Philip Kotler: *Marketing Management*, 11th Edition.

3

Ancient Wisdom and Business Ethics

Dr Vaneeta Rani and Dr Kusum Gupta

Introduction

Social issues in business have a long history while ethical issues have suddenly gained status. The word "ethics" was once considered irrelevant by corporate loyalists, but now discussion of it is increasingly seen as not only important but also as critical to a company's success. Till the 1990s Indian corporations regarded business ethics as a mere extension of philanthropy. Although corporate giants like Tatas and Birlas contributed generously to philanthropic causes, it was only after the entry of MNCs in the Indian market that the definition of business ethics has broadened from the concept of philanthropy. The word "ethics" is derived from the Latin word "ethicus" and the Greek word "ethikos," which means ideal standards of human behaviour. Simplify defined, ethics means moral principles which influence or control one's behaviour and point to whether a particular action is good or bad, in terms of the welfare of others.

Points of Comment

1. **Ethics differ from society to society.** For instance, artificial birth control is mandatory in Russia and China; but a taboo (a cultural or religious custom that does not allow people to do a particular thing) in Catholic Christian soceties.
2. **Ethics differ from religion to religion.** For instance, in some religions meat-eating is strictly prohibited and regarded as highly unethical; whereas in some religions meat-eating is not at all prohibited and is considered most ethical according to religious standards and values.
3. **Ethics differ from time to time.** For instance, in ancient times, the phenomenon of women taking up jobs in business and other enterprises was regarded as unethical; but in the present-day-times this notion has changed and women taking up outside jobs are most welcome in society.

Philosophers viewed ethics as system of moral principles and the methods for applying them. It deals with values relating to human conduct with respect to the right and wrong of certain actions and to the goodness and badness of the motives and ends of such actions. While others consider emerging ethical beliefs to be "State of Act" legal matters, i.e. what is an ethical guideline today is often translated to a law or regulation. Business can be defined as a primary economic institution through which people in modern societies carry on the task of producing and distributing goods and services. And business ethics refers to the application of ethical judgments to business activities. Business ethics explains that business can generate profits by being ethical. But this thought (business ethics) till last decade was being contradicted. Due to expansion of business, the application of ethical practices and its implications has created a need for practicing business ethics. Today more and more importance is being given to the application of ethical practices in business dealings and the ethical implications of business decisions.

Human beings have the ability to choose. When choice is provided between right and wrong or good and bad, an individual chooses one of the alternatives by distinguishing between the options available. This concept applies to business. Since businesses are operated by human beings, they should be able to distinguish between right or wrong decisions in their business. Thus, businesses also have choices or alternatives, such as to maximise profits, increase sales volume, provide employee benefits and concern for society. However, at times profits and social responsibility cannot coexist. Because, while earning profits entrepreneurs may neglect social responsibility. For instance, some chemical firms driven by profit motive may postpone investment in social welfare projects like Effluent Treatment Plant (ETP), although the industrial waste left into the environment in hazardous to public health. Thus, it becomes difficult to maximise both profits and social responsibility. This situation results in a managerial dilemma. Where managers have to choose between profits and for the organisation and social consideration towards the community.

At times, business finds it difficult to explain its action on ethical grounds. For instance, banks' decision to computerise their activities to provide spontaneous quality service to meet customer requirements may result in redundancy of clerical jobs. The ethical solution lies in job reassignment or retraining for alternative job assignments. Any business, if it wants to survive and grow in the long run must strike a balance between its social obligations and economic objectives. These obligations may be complex and costly to discharge. But if the organisation wants to be ethical, it has to discharge its social obligations towards the society on the basis of ethical concepts.

Thus business ethics can be defined as moral principles which must govern the conduct of business enterprises; and guide businessmen as to whether their decision and actions are right and wrong in terms of the welfare of the society.

Business Ethics through Indian Scriptures

India is a country of high values and ethics. It is land where people of all religions and cultures, with difference in languages, beliefs, social background live together. We see that the various scriptures written by great men of ancient times, of all religious backgrounds, speak more or less of the same concepts. Also, all their teachings, preaching and writings can provide as a guide for "Effective and Ethical Management." In the present world where "making profit" at any cost is the main motive, and where people opine that "either you can ethical or do business"; these teachings from the holy books and other scriptures are a good answer to them, guiding us how both Ethics and Business can go together.

The Ramayana: One can easily co-relate the modern-say management lessons with Lord Rama's teaching in "Ramayana". Lord Rama presents the masterpiece example of "Leading by Value". How a manager has to tackle the situations is well presented by him. When Vibhishana asks him how will he defeat this huge army with his limited resources, he explains using the example of a chariot, whose four wheels denote: character, courage, ethics and valour; the four horses denote: gusto, strength, energy and passion: and their four reins denote: forgiveness, compassion, consistency and equanimity. Thus, the weaponry: knowledge, strategy, intelligence, skills, commitment and a restraint of ego these are the weapons which can help us win any kind of battle. "Emotional Intelligence an embodiment of all these things mentioned above is what makes victory possible against any opposition. You need to be consistent in your approach to different people, no matter whom they are and where they are coming from. Ramayana gives us example of a "good manager" in Rama, Sugriva, Vibhishana and that of a "bad manager" in Ravana. A good manager is one who can even get his work done from his rivals as we can take for instance; Angad (whose father was killed by Rama) actually helped in battle. This shows the excellent managerial skill of Rama and Sughriva while Ravana being a "bad" one, continuously ignored the suggestions of his managers, including Vibhishana, and lost the battle and his kingdom. Other aspects of modern-day management can be seen by: the "High Motivation" provided by Jamvant to Hanuman when he had forgotten his powers: "Swot analysis" is done by Hanuman in analysing the strength, weaknesses, opportunities and threats of the Lankan army, when he was asked to convey Rama's message to Goddess Sita; the "Strategic Alliance" formed by Lord Rama and Sugriva in which the former helped in regaining his lost kingdom while the latter helped in providing resources and help find Sita and win overt Ravana. Businesses are run on relations and Lord Rama in Ramayana has proved that a manager who can nurture good relations with the employees, clients, and anyone in whose contact the organisation and the management comes in, can do wonders in the company.

2. The Holy Quran: The Holy Quran also sets out the institutional framework for achieving promised results. Various ayats in the Holy Quran guide us how ethical concepts are implied in modern-day management. Obedience and respect for authority is the basic fundamental requisite. It is necessary for those people who are given the job to complete a task to obey all legal and reasonable orders and perform it reasonably, as Holy Quran instructs in this ayat: *[4:59]* "Obey Allah and his Messenger and those in position of authority among you." The importance of "joint consultation" and "team work" is also revealed by the Quran. As in the following ayat: *[3:159]* "pass over (their faults), and ask for (God's) forgiveness for them: and consult them in affairs (of moment). Then, when you have taken a decision put your trust in God, for God loves those who put their trust (in Him)." The Holy Quran also puts forth the principle of "equal opportunities" which relates to modern management as all members of an organisation shall have equal and fair chances to grow, contribute, and be rewarded accordingly. This is presented in the ayat: "O people we created you from a single male and female couple and then divided you in nations and tribes so that you may recognise one another. Verily the most honourable among you in the sight of Allah is he who is most "righteous" of you." Also, speaking about the "Elimination of wastage", the ayat: *[17:26]* of the Holy Quran: 'And render to the kindred their due rights, as (also) to those in want, and to the wayfarer. But waste not (your wealth, time, health, talents, opportunities etc) in the manner of a spendthrift."

3. The Holy Bible: As mentioned earlier, the corporate definition of ethics lies in knowing about actions that are good and bad and also treating the stakeholders with respect. The teachings of Jesus Christ and the Ten Commandants as given in the Bible, has significant impact on business ethics. These can be illustrated in the following verses of the Bible: "Do into others as you would have them do to you" has the underlying lessons for the businesses that they should treat their stakeholders by the business operation with the respect and honestly that they would like those people to show to them. "Love the neighbour"; neighbour, in terms of business, are those who work in the organisation itself (they are the closest "neighbours" of the business). The term "love" in this verse refers to forming the basis of the family type of cultural environment that many businesses strive to achieve in the workplace. Good businesses succeed because of the ethical bond they form with employees. "Thou shalt not bear false witness", "thou shalt not steal"; these verses present the ethical value of "honesty and trust". All researchers promote the values of honesty and trust as being critical to the building of business relationships. Honesty in terms of advertising, marketing, financial issues and the like are of sheer importance.

In addition to the above, the influence that the Bible has upon ethical business practices is also dependent upon the individuals who lead the organisation. It is not the fact that the ethical values might be incorporated within the business code of practice, but also they will have to see these values reinforced in practice.

4. The Bhagvad Gita: The guidelines, teachings and values taught by Lord Krishna to Arjuna during the battle of the Mahabharata are contained in the Bhagvad Gita. The modern management concepts like vision, leadership, motivation, excellence in work, achieving goals, meaning of work, attitude towards work, nature of individual, decision-making, planning etc., are all discussed in the Bhagavad Gita with a sharp insight. When Duryodhana and Arjuna were asked to choose among Lord Krishna's army or his knowledge; Duryodhana went for his large army while Arjuna went for his wisdom. This shows that in terms of "resources", a manager must choose wisely and utilise optimally just as Arjuna did. Gita also tells us about the "commitment towards work" through the law of detachment. By titling the performance towards the anticipated benefits, the quality of performance of the present duty suffers on account of the mental agitations caused by the anxieties of the future. The very popular Shloka 47 of chapter 2 in the Bhagvad Gita, ("Karmanya Vadhikaraste ma phleshu kadaachan, / ma Kampala heturbhrma te sango astav akamani"). Your right is only to do your duty, and not to its fruit or result. Neither the result of your action should be your motive, nor should you become inactive". In Chapter 16 of the Gita Sri Krishna elaborates on two types of Work Ethic viz. daivi sampat or divine work culture means fearlessness, purity, self-control, sacrifice, straightforwardness, self-denial, calmless, absence of fault-finding, absence of greed, gentleness, modesty, absence of envy and pride; and asuri sampat or demonic work culture means egotism, delusion, desire-centric, improper performance, work which is not oriented towards service. This principle explains that mere "work ethic" is not enough in as much as a hardened criminal has also a very good work culture. What is needed is a "work ethic" conditioned by "ethics in work". Henry Fayol, mentioned among his principles, "subordination of individual interest to general interest". This is well depicted in Shlokas 31-38 of Chapter 2 in which Lord Krishna guides Arjuna to fight "not for his own benefits, not for satisfying his own greed or desire, but for the good of many". Krishna also advises, in regard to temporary failures, "No doer of good ever ends in misery". Every action should produce results: good action produces good results and evil begets nothing but evil. So, one should always act well and be rewarded. Apart from helping humans in self-discovery, Gita eulogizes Karma i.e. human endeavour of action (Karma Yoga) is better than renunciation of action (Karma Sanyasa).

Relationship between Business and Ethics

As mentioned by management guru Peter Drucker, "More and more people in the workforce- and mostly knowledge workers- will have to manage themselves." The average working life is likely to be fifty years for knowledge workers. But the average life expectancy of successful business is only about thirty years. If they want to survive for long, they will have to change their structure, their work, their knowledge and the kind of people they employ. While the knowledge workers need to identify themselves, their strengths, the way they work, and their contribution. Today, the culture that facilitates psychological and spiritual development of the individual and community besides creating a cohesive community which co-ordinates the creativity, well-being, self realisation, and inner outer unity of a person with himself and with the stakeholders, environment, society and the humanity as a whole.

Classical thinkers like Adam Smith were of the opinion that the objective of any business was to generate profits only, and business had no relationship with ethics. While other thinkers expressed that neither the business was an extension of morality and ethics, nor can business keep itself far away from ethical practices of the society where it exists and operates. The various views regarding the relationship of business and ethics are as follows.

1. The Unitarian View of Ethics

According to the Unitarian view, business is a part of moral ethics. If businesses want to exist, survive and flourish in the long-run, morality and ethics cannot be separated from the operation of the business. The view also emphasises that business should concentrate on society and it has a major role to play in serving the society and ushering in society welfare.

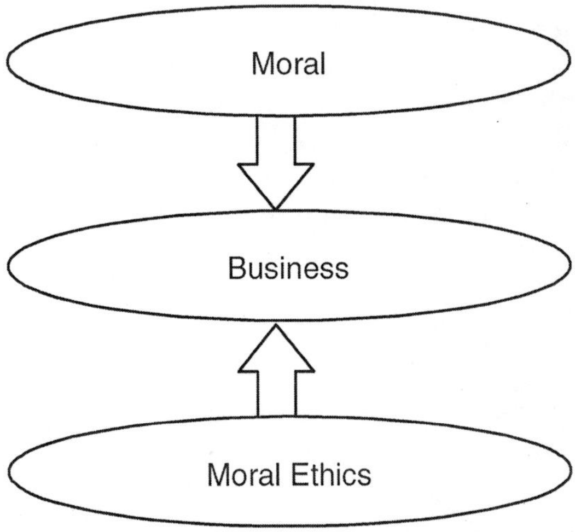

Fig. 1. The Unitarian View of Ethics.

2. The Separatist View of Ethics

Classical economists like Adam Smith and Milton Friedman proposed the separatist view. They were of the opinion that businesses in order to flourish should concentrate on their goal-profit maximisation. Morality and ethics, they argued, have no role in business. Milton Friedman was of the opinion that business should concentrate on production and distribution of goods and service. Social problems are to be tackled by the government and concerned individual, but not by the firms or businesses. In short, the only aim of business is to generate profits. According to Adam Smith, business is a distinct entity and does not include ethics and morality. If ethics were introduced in business, it would lead to imbalance of market dynamics. This view lays emphasis on business concerns like reducing production costs, optimising labour etc. These concerns are relevant to the marketplace, not to ethical and moral issues.

Many intellectuals believe that if ethics morality were given an opportunity to enter into the business arena, then there is a danger of social values dominating over business values. And this replacement may ruin the efficiency of the business. These intellectuals also believed that business should concentrate on profits, and managers should manage or concentrate on the interests of the shareholders. Shareholders should be given the opportunity in deciding about the effective utilisation of resources. In other words, business should focus on achieving its economic objectives.

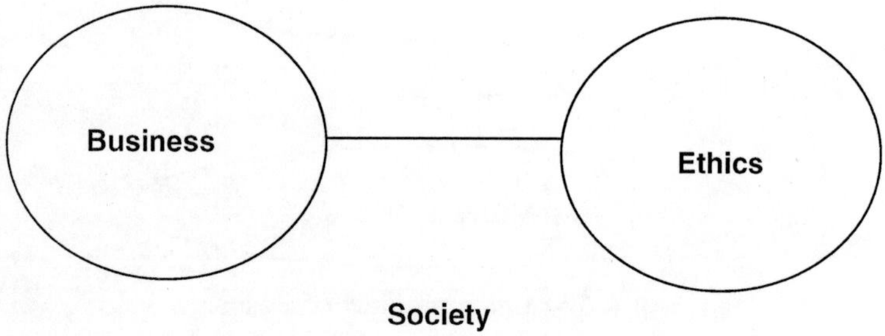

Fig. 2. The Separatist View of Ethics.

3. The Integration View of Ethics

Talcott Persons proposed a view called the integration view. He was of the opinion that ethical behaviour and business should be integrated or combined in a new area called 'Business Ethics'. He argued that business being economic entity, has the right to make profits, but at the same time it should discharge the social obligation. According to this view, business and morality are inter-related and are guided by external factors like government, market system, law, law and society. The government and market system are related to business i.e. rules laid down by the government directly or indirectly affect the business, and may thus affect the market system. Similarly, laws will guide business, and decide what is right or wrong in the business.

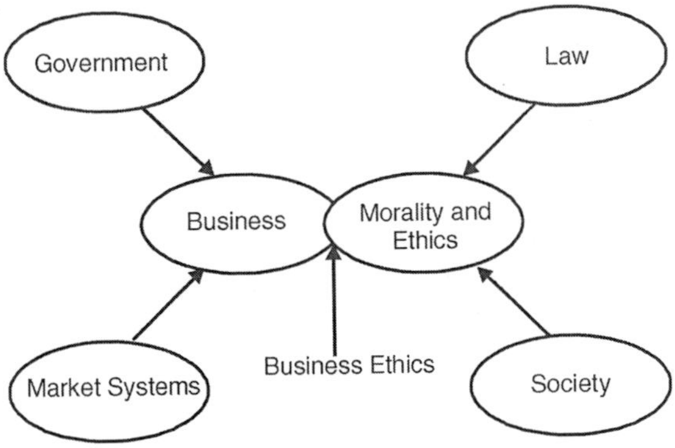

Fig. 3. The Integration View of Ethics.

Stages of Ethical Consciousness in Business

Ethical standards vary between cultures and countries. These variations are more evident among entrepreneurs or corporations in a given nation. One can better understand these variations if the different levels of ethical consciousness in business are well-defined. It has been found that moral (ethical) development follows a specific sequence of stage, irrespective of cultures and countries. In the business context, the stage of ethical consciousness is as follows:

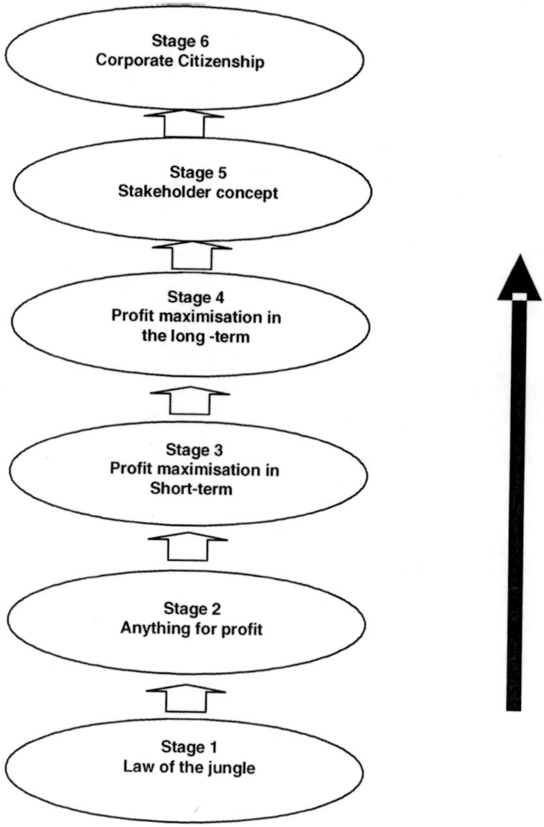

In the first stage, businesses were run on brute strength; business decisions were driven by the philosophy of "might makes right." Business ills like price fixing etc were common in this stage.

In the second stage of "Anything for profit." Business was ready to do anything to make a profit. Businesses at this stage had only one goal i.e. profit. To generate profits, businesses resorted to false representation of products, bribery of government officials, tax evasion etc. Business in this stage of ethical consciousness strongly believed that "anything goes as long as one does not get caught by the law or by the customer."

In the third stage, maximising profits in the short-term, businesses operated on the socially and generally accepted business practices. In this stage, business believed that "good business is good ethics". The performance of business was measured based on short-term growth in sales and profits. The main aim of business in this stage was to maximise profits within the constraints of the law.

In the fourth stage, maximising profits in the long-run, saw a shift in focus from "business" to "ethics". In this level ethical consciousness, businesses knowledge that "sound ethics is good business" in the long run. Although the interest of the shareholders remained the primary concern of businesses, there was equal concern for conducting business in a manner that was both "right" and which would also prove to be profitable over the longer term, even if other alternatives might produce greater short-term profits. At this stage of consciousness firms created the post of an "ethics officer" to supervise the ethical aspect of the business.

In the fifth stage, "stakeholders concept" companies concentrated on profits which had a social as well as economic mission. In this stage business objectives included profit sharing, development of community service projects, and philanthropy. The driving assumption of this concept is that business wanted to strike a balance between providing a service to stakeholders and working towards the good of society. The focus at this stage was on building and maintaining mutually enabling relationships, which in turn created value for others and justified the firm's profit. Success was measured not just in financial terms but also in terms of contribution of society. Some companies have gone so far as to publish regular annual social reports similar to their annual financial reports.

The sixth stage, "Corporate Citizenship," proposes a higher level of ethical consciousness and redefine the mission of business in society. The World Business Academy and Business for Social Responsibility, both associations and networks of business leaders, are among the principal proponents of the higher level of ethical consciousness. This "social responsibility" school of thought also present in Stage Five, but to a lesser degree, maintains that business has a major responsibility to contribute to the necessary transformation of what they consider to be a very unhealthy society today. Their belief is based on the premise that a business can be healthy only if society around it is healthy and that no other institution in society, including governments and religious institutions, has the resources of the credibility to bring about this transformation. Entrepreneurs operating on this level would seek to achieve certain social objectives such as promoting community health, participating in job creation, employing handicapped people, and self-realisation of employees as well as financial success of the company.

Conclusion

The above discussion shows that important aspects of Management and Business Ethics can be discovered from our scriptures. We have seen many people advocating the concept that one can do either business or ethics. But this is not the fact. Good actions always yield good results. One may say that Jesus Christ was crucified even after being righteous but the real fact is that his teachings and lessons are being followed even today and he is worshipped by so many people. At the end of the millennium, we are back to basics. Even as society appears to be getting increasingly corrupt and criminal; many are beginning to realise that you cannot aspire to create value without deeply cherishing a sense of values. Thus, it is rightly said that "Ethics and religion must not stay at home when we go to work." The study also expressed the views of various economists regarding the relationship between business and ethics. This resulted in three different views: Unitarian view, Separatist view and Integration view. Unitarian view argues that morality and ethics are related to business. The Separatist view expressed that, business should concentrate on profits, and ethics and morality do not form a part of business. The Integration view defined a new area called business ethics, where ethical behaviour and business are integrated. The external forces like government, market system, law and services will guide the ethical behaviour of the business. Thus, this paper discusses the need or necessity for business ethics - business in order to survive in the long run should concentrate on the welfare of society.

4

Dream of an Ethical Society and the Dilemma of Capitalism

Dr Sheojee Singh

Introduction

The present phase of human civilisation is beset with multiple transitional stages and the dilemma of ethics is one of such essential challenges of the present phase of life. Wealth management or resources management is an essential need today, yet its consequent deviants need to be minimised. This paper attempts to analyse this prominent dilemma of our time in a logical and scientific way thereby providing a deeper insight into this and other related issues which adversely affect our happiness-index in day to day living. The author stresses the fact that the dream of an ethical society has been very dear to human imagination since time immemorial and it became a social necessity with the onward march of civilisation, but the conflicting demands put on the individual from various quarters of the immediate environment create a whirlpool of choices in action. The freedom of choice is limited yet the dream of an ethical society can be realised if the individual as well as the group tries to adhere to the clarion call of *'Ten Tyaktena Bhunjithah'* of the Upanishad. Reviewing some researches in the related areas, the author presents, through this paper, a tentative programme of resources-management whereby prosperity can be achieved through service-oriented approach. Quoting from the Indian classics like the Upanishads, the Bhagavad Gita and the Ramacharitamanas, it has been asserted in this paper how ethical conduct can be promoted through community involvement and corporate social responsibility. Referring to some studies worldwide on human welfare and capital generation, the author concludes that capitalism as such is not at fault, but the over-crowding of the inner space of human psyche is the root cause of poverty of striving for excellence towards righteousness (*Yogah Karmashu Kaushalam*-Bhagavad Gita, Ch-2), which we name as corruptibility.

Ethics and Human Society

When man started living in a group, there was a need to regulate the behaviour of group members so that nobody felt uncomfortable and everyone gets equal chances to grow harmoniously to his/ her full potential in life. This pattern of regulatory behaviour started the concept of some code of conduct, which later got modified into ethics. The concept of an ideal society is based the observance of ethical principles of living by every individual with an aim to overcome the so-called human limitations and reach a state of harmony in life so as to manifest the inherent divinity of the human race. Ethics are the eternal principles of righteous living, individually as well as collectively. The idea of economic independence and prosperity is not the one of accumulating the resources for fulfilling our needs and fanning our greeds for a long period of time. On the contrary, it is for preparing us to enjoy the earthly life through increasing spirit of renunciation amidst prosperity in the true spirit of the Upanishads-*'Ten Tyaktena Bhunjithah Enjoy thy wealth by renouncing it)'*.

Economics and Ethics - A Contradiction or Complement?

Whenever we talk of economic development, we generally talk in terms of wealth management and distribution among and for a particular class/ group of people. The basic philosophy of wealth generation for the larger good of the masses has taken a back seat and the driving force behind the present economic order has become the principle of profit by any means, even by exploiting painfully the very people for whom it intends to exist. There seems no end to the exploitative machinery of the global economy in the near future and its impact is badly felt by one and all today. From the simple farmers in villages to the sophisticated economic players in the Wall Street, everyone is feeling the heat now. The economy seems to threaten its own very basis. A world in crisis is desperately looking towards better ethical alternatives for solving its recurring problems amidst its trial and error approach to create a generous capitalist economy.

A large portion of revenue is generated by the sale of liquor and associated addictive materials and the plea is given that this revenue will be used for social sectors affecting the lives of the so-called underprivileged in a positive way. The ethical considerations are thrown to the wind in the process. The vicious cycle continues and suffering grows in proportion. A poet has nicely described the situation in the following couplets:

'Kabhi Nahi Lag sakta Yaron mayakhane me tala
Ek -do -teen- char nahi, sara shahar hai pinewala'

(the liquor shop cannot be closed as not one, two, three but the whole town is drunkard)

More and more people become addicted to alcohol and other bad habits and the problems continue to increase in quality and quantity. The saying proves correct - *'Jas jas Suarasa Badan badhava tahi dun kapi badanaa badhava'.*

Emergence of Capitalism

The lust for accumulating more and more of resources and valuing oneself in terms of just the day to day emergency needs started a movement for capital formation.

The modern capitalist economy has given exclusive emphasis on wealth generation by exploiting natural and human resources. The result has been increasing mechanisation and corporatisation of life without due regards to basic human values. This economic order is heading from crisis to crisis with just fire fighting mechanisms to contain the damage to a tolerable level. But the fact is that if the system demands a basic change in its frame of reference, it cannot be brought about just by some superficial and cosmetic adjustments. What we need today is the rethinking about the very structural basis of our economy. Economics is not just a science of wealth generation but also a science of enhancing human welfare. But the market economy is based on creating artificial want for largely unwanted things in the larger section of population in order to get the mass-scale produced goods consumed indiscriminately and then create a vicious cycle of flawed demand-supply network in which humanity seems entangled. People are made to understand that earning a lot of money is the only purpose of their life. The whole life is geared to accumulation of wealth in order to fulfill the pseudo-needs of the individuals and societies. In the rat race of wealth-accumulation, we forget to adhere to the ethical principles of life and the consequent domination of brute forces in our daily life makes our life hellish. It is no wonder then that life loses its wonder and the charisma of creative living is out of our reach. In the words of Oliver Goldsmith, 'Where wealth accumulates, and men decay'.

Capitalist View of Life and Resources

Capitalism views everything in terms of economic gains and losses. People are viewed as resources and their active participation in resource mobilisation moves. In fact, it has separated the concept of well being from that of affluence. It has slowly started dehumanising the individuals and society at the same time in pursuit of material affluence.

Achievements of Capitalism

It has ensured material prosperity and hunger-free world for the new generation. We have been able to live in bigger homes, enjoy better amenities of life and create an environment for the material development of a large portion of humanity. It has pumped money in various production processes leading to fulfillment of basic needs of man. It has also helped man to dream better and use improved techniques to realise that dream. Yet, on the whole, it does not seem to help mankind improve its lot fundamentally. Now, let us see to what extent it has been able to ensure human welfare.

Capitalism and Human Welfare

Initially, the management of resources was the main focus, but along with that activity, human welfare was also ensured to a large extent. Although capitalism achieved much by way of industrialisation, it came to be marked by a high degree of inequality in distribution of wealth and income, by economic instability, by trade cycles, by unemployment and, in general a great deal of social injustice and exploitation.[1] The importance of ethics was disregarded in such a scenario. In fact, the exclusive concern of economics has been economic growth indicated by a higher GDP and there is hardly any concern for simultaneous growth in human well-being. As Fullbrook (2004) points out that "the economists (read market economists) do not confuse economic growth with growth in the well being and that if others confuse it that has nothing to do with them; the current measure of GDP is not designed for gauging the human well being and that the economists and experts in national accounting devote 100 per cent of their efforts in measuring and using GDP and economic growth instead of directing only 50 per cent of their efforts in that direction and reserving the other 50 per cent for developing and designing alternative indicators that better reflect notions of well being, human development, social development, sustainable development etc". Actually, the problem with market economy lies in its very foundation of exclusive concern for wealth generation disregarding the ultimate purpose of its effort. Human welfare hardly finds a place in its scheme of economic activities.

Capitalism and Human Suffering

Capitalism has started indirect wars among a group of people termed as suppliers and consumers. The various sectors of capitalist economy aim at maximising profit even at the cost of welfare of the other side, for example, the consumer goods and services. This has further resulted in a loss of faith in the goodness of the system, which further leads to untold suffering for all concerned. Each party wants to play smart over the other and cut throat competition becomes the rule of the game.

Almost everything is being decided by the projections and trends of the market. The individuality of a person is getting lost in the crowd of madness for money-power. Insanity has taken the driving seat in journey of human life and the golden rule of contentment in human life has become outdated. Various kinds of pulls and pressures make life full of tension and resultant depression. The joy of righteous living has become a thing of the past for most of us. Ethics, which used to be guiding force for human beings until recently, have become the things of a forgotten past. Talking of ethics and ethical living is considered a sign of backwardness today. Trying to lead a contented life guided by ethics and values is a crime today. Self-deception and so-called smartness have become the laws of life. The increasing self-centredness of man is spoiling human relations and social life has become another name for crowd-mentality without the feeling of togetherness. Everyone seems to be in hurry to ensure a reasonable means of livelihood for the longest possible period of time but nobody bothers about the ways and means of life and living. Every individual human being seems to be lost in wilderness.

Some Research Studies

Studies (Tooley, J. 2010; Krishna, A., 2009) carried out in about 139 developing nation-states illustrate how capitalism has created the hunger for more and more wealth without any substantial way reducing the poverty of society as a whole. The gap between the haves and have-nots has increased over the years manifold. The most disturbing consequence has been the erosion of faith in togetherness for solving individual as well as collective problems.

Capitalism and the Conflict of Interests

The major issue with capitalism is how it can help us explore the interests, help us exploit the resources and make us confident in tackling the problems related to our material life. No doubt, it has contributed substantially to that end and reduced the incidences of want from a large number of people by supplying the needed resources in time, yet the general trend it has set in has far more debilitating consequences than material want and poverty.

Most of the people are sinking into misery, while a few are enjoying a life of luxury. Global inequalities, corruption, apathy, indifference to the human feelings and insensitiveness have become the hallmark of societies today all over the world.

Societies the world over are witnessing the breaking of basic family structure, which is more apparent and devastating in the Indian context. This has resulted into a disturbing chain reaction for the new generation, which segregates man from man. Patience, perseverance, fellow-feeling, sensitivity, consideration for others and most important of all, a sense of space and relaxation for oneself and the sacredness of life hardly find a place in the present scheme life. And without these ingredients in place, it is next to impossible for human beings to enjoy the bounties of nature. Life today has become totally mechanical for most of us.

Capitalism and the Classical Dilemma

The age old dilemma of perception of the haves and have-nots regarding wealth creation, management and distribution along with the interpretative understanding of human needs and greed has remained the classical dilemma of mankind over the last many centuries. The economic theories propounded, propagated and applied in various aspects of human life for the last almost about three centuries assert that capitalism has remained a fast forward and powerful economic philosophy for ensuring mass scale material prosperity, yet the untold suffering accrued to a large number of people because of the vested interests created by the same philosophy goes against the very aim of creating an ethically sound socio-economic set up for man.

Social cohesion is missing because of the over-indulgence of man in the process of production owing to the dictates of market-economy. There is an increasing sense of alienation among the various constituents of society. The war is set in very subtle form and the society willingly forgets its own role to provide a conducive environment for *flowering of goodness* in man. The *response potential* of man is getting weakened and dulled with every passing day. People are physically living together but are hardly concerned for one another. Self-centredness is increasing and there is a feeling of void amongst individuals. Everybody feels the other to be a market factor, either guided by demand or supply. Humanity is slowly losing its humane touch and it is one of the most disturbing contributions of market economy that every body seems busy but actually busy for nothing significant in life. Human values are getting neglected.

Individuals hardly value eternal values of life for its own sake. Everything seems to be at the command of the market forces. If something is marketable, it has value otherwise not. The use and throw fashion has become the *mantra* of life. Humanity has got entangled in economic wilderness.

Kalam puts it beautifully: 'perhaps there is so much conflict between peoples and nations because in our pursuit of prosperity and power, we have lost sight of ethical values.'

The social impact of market economy has really become disturbing. The growing alienation of man from himself, his surrounding nature, the immediate human concerns and the search for reality has created some of the following disastrous consequences-

1. Breaking of families and family ties.
2. Increasing sense of indifference among the individuals.
3. Lack of trust and trustworthiness.
4. General feeling of inadequacy/ insufficiency and growing discontent in life.
5. Decreasing social cohesion.
6. Increasing mechanisation of life.
7. Increasing instances of corruption in public life.
8. Degeneration of moral and spiritual values.
9. Growing tension and depression.
10. Disappearance of the traditional rural societies and economies.
11. Increasing corporate culture.
12. Disappearance of the innocence of childhood, carefree energy of the youth and godly detached compassion of the elders.
13. Increasing cleverness and decreasing simplicity of life.
14. Growing need for economic security as a primary source of happiness in life.

15. Exploitation of nature beyond the point of return.
16. De-spiritualisation of life and so on.

Thus we find that the above mentioned disturbing social impact of a market economy has troubled mankind a lot and there does not appear any viable alternative to mitigate the suffering of man in near future in the present economic philosophy of life.

The Way Out of the Dilemma: Vedantic Worldview

The dilemma is most appropriately analys in the Vedantic worldview by Sri Aurobindo in his magnum opus *Life Divine*. Even a leading economist of our time, Professor Datta (2012) asserts, "A society may be technically advanced, it may have obliterated illiteracy, its members may possess discipline and a number of other civic virtues, yet it may fee inwardly hollow or be afflicted by a growing sense of loneliness or spiritual insignificance; as the ethics of industrialisation and capitalism is not the sufficient basis for whole living."

Urbanisation, industrialisation and mass production of goods as well as services were to be causes of human degeneration. At the centre of ethical economy is the ethico-spiritual man, who does not live by bread alone but is capable of producing his own bread and butter with the help of immediate environment in non-exploitative way and is strong enough to share his wealth for the welfare of all. The essence and culmination of this economy consists in freeing man from wants and creating the true brotherhood of man (*Vasudhaiva Kutumbakam*) as an essence of world peace and development of a globally inspiring model of human development.

Integrating the Better of the Two Approaches - The Scientific Spiritualism

Now, when we see the above analysis in the light of scientific findings, we come to what may be termed as scientific spiritualism. Herein the merits of capitalism are retained with greater awareness of social responsibility and the sense of ethics. The ethical dilemma is resolved with the help of a larger perspective and long-term planning. The guiding principle then is not the maximisation of profit anyway but the welfare of maximum number of people through ensuring active participation of the maximum number of people in their own upliftment with righteous use of available resources. It should be an enabling kind of mechanism rather than feeder one, which helps each man in his unique process of development in harmony with the world within and without.

The Way to Prosperity: India's Seminal Contribution

The way to prosperity in Indian thinking is through service and renunciation. Contentment has been regarded as the greatest wealth in Indian thinking (*Santosham Param Dhanam*). As Sri Aurobindo points out: "All the problems of existence are essentially problems of harmony", unless there is a harmony among the various dimensions of life of an individual, any plan for human happiness will have limited significance. If we want fulfillment and joy in life, which have become a historical fact for a major portion of humanity, there is no other way. If we want the rampant corruption, wanton killing and widespread distrust and indifference (which have come as a package deal with exclusive material prosperity) to vanish from the individual and collective living, then there is no other way- *'Nanyo panthah Vidyate anayay'*. If we want our life to be inwardly and outwardly beautiful and harmonious, we have to resort to the true spirit of ethical living making our life a means to self-realisation.

Conclusion

Thus, we can assert in conclusion that capitalism being guided by corporate social responsibility and greater awareness of its limitations in facilitating happiness of all through wealth generation, can bring true prosperity to mankind. In words of Sri Aurobindo:

"The force of man can be driven by God's force
Then is he a miracle doing miracles
For only so can he be Nature's king."

We can conclude by quoting from Marglin (2008): "Economists celebrate the market as a device for regulating human interaction without acknowledging that their enthusiasm depends on a set of half truths: that individuals are autonomous, self-interested, rational calculators with unlimited wants and that the only community that matters is the nation-state. However, market relationships erode other forms of community. In the past, for example, people supported each other in adversity. A fire or illness was an occasion on which the community pitched in. Now if my house burns down, or I become disabled, I turn not to my neighbours but to my insurance company. Insurance may be a more efficient way to organise resources than a community engaging in mutual help, but the deep social and human ties that are constitutive of community are weakened by the shift from reciprocity to market relations." We can thus say that for modern man to live in harmony with the world outside and at peace within oneself, the best alternative seems to make our capitalist economy geared to human welfare instead of its present pre-occupation with wealth manipulation. This can be best achieved through Gandhian ethics being incorporated as the guiding principles of our economic activities. Corporate Social Responsibility seems one better step in this direction. As things stand today, we cannot revert to the model of *Gram Swarjya* of Gandhiji overnight, but it is within our hands to adopt, in spirit, the principles of individual as well as collective living rooted in Gandhian ethics for enrichment and fulfillment in life. In words of Sriman Narayan, this will ensure not just raising the *standard of our living* but also the *standard of life*.

References

Datta A. (2012): *Development-Challenges and Responses* Vol.1, p. 299., Divya Jeevan Prakashan, Gurgaon, Haryana, India.

Vinoba (1981): Thoughts on Education; Sarva Seva Sangha, Rajghat Varanasi, pp. 14-15.

Sri Aurobindo (1939): Life Divine, Sri Aurobindo Ashram Press, Pondicherry, pp. 22-23.

Gandhi, M.K.(1908): Hind Swaraj; Navjeevan Press, Ahmedabad, pp. 12-15.

Sri Aurobindo (1950): Savitri, Sri Aurobindo Ashram Press, Pondicherry.

Krishna, A.(2010): One Illness Away, Oxford University Press, New Delhi.

Tooley, J.(2009): The Beautiful Tree, Penguin Books (India), New Delhi.

5

Faith and Spirituality in an Increasingly Global Business Environment

Renu Kalra and Rakhi J. Singh

Introduction

Today's unstable economy puts added stress on leaders and individuals in the workplace. When leaders are stressed, maintaining their values becomes more difficult. There is evidence that many modern managers are discovering and rediscovering the importance of a spiritual dimension in their work lives and in their work relationships. Psychologists, sociologists, management gurus and business leaders have begun to argue for the importance of exploring faith and spirituality at workplace. Corporations and individuals show a steadily increasing interest in creating organisations that nurture the human spirit. Yet, walk into almost any organisation these days and you still find fear anger, resistance to change, dishonesty, and disbelief. The best employees are usually looking to go somewhere else and the employees who are not so marketable are trying to stay under the radar and just hand on for dear life. Is this a formula for growth high productivity or high performance? Is this the way to create a sustainable organisation- certainly not?

The earliest management theories were developed by people in the early twentieth with an engineering approach. At that time, the focus was on the physical effectiveness and efficiency of workers. F.W. Taylor saw the human body as an extension of the machine and studied ways to utilise the human machine with as little wasted energy and motion as possible. The next phase of management thought came out of the Hawthorne studies in the 1930s and 40s. These studies concluded that emotional and social needs were just as important to high performance as physical efficiency. The next evolution of management theory occurred in the 1970s and throughout the 90s with the advent of the quality movement and the movement towards greater employee participation and involvement in the work (Juran, 1964; During 1986). Researchers and practitioners began to value the intellectual capabilities of workers and to see them as the experts on their own jobs. With the quality and participation moment, employees were put into teams and asked to define and solve work-related problems and implement solutions to improve organisational outcomes in a measurable way. But until the early 1990s there was essentially no acknowledgement that the human spirit plays an important role in the workplace with the exception of Robert Greenleaf and his work on *Servant Leadership* (1977). Three of the Four Key Human energies were acknowledged in management theory and practice.

1. Physical energy
2. Emotional
3. Intellectual energy, but the fourth
4. Spiritual energy - was seen as nonexistent at worst or not relevant at best.

As the concept of what it means to be human is expanding, so too are our management theories expanding. Interest in the workplace spirituality has increased steadily in the new millennium. This is especially reflected in the number of special issues/books on spirituality, religion and management that have been published in academic journals such as *Leadership Quarterly* (2003, 14 (6), *Organisation* 2003, 10(2), *Megatrends* 2010, *The Soul of Business, Liberating the Corporate Soul, Working from the Heart, What would the Buddha do at Work?* etc. In short, some evidence exists that suggests a link between workplace spirituality and enhanced individual creativity.

Signs of this sudden concern for corporate soul are showing up everywhere, from boardrooms to company lunchrooms, from business conferences newsletters, from management consulting firms to business schools.

This new century's task will be to rediscover its "Gods"- Echoing Andre Maring.

Organisations increasingly realise how shortsighted it is to focus solely on financial success at the cost of humanistic values (Galen and West, 1995). In the modern world, we have evolved a culture that separates man's spiritual life from his institutional life. This turn of events has had a far reaching impact on modern organisations. Our companies freely may claim to mind and muscle, but they are culturally discouraged from intruding upon our personal lives and deeper beliefs.

What we need is a non-defined, non-religious "Spiritualism" that enables a firm's subordinate to respond truly to the inner meaning that many people seek in their work - or alternatively, seek in their lives and could find at work. As James Autry observed, work can provide the opportunity for spiritual and personal, as well as financial growth. If it does not, we are wasting far too much of our lives on it. Leading others is now seen as an extension of managing ourselves. The implications of this change are clear. On the one hand, it is about working collectively reflectively and spiritually smarter, on the other hand it implies employment that is mind enriching, heart fulfilling, soul satisfying as well as financial rewarding.

Defining Spirituality Passion

It is interesting to note, that while the attention to workplace spirituality is indeed growing there is debate as to what exactly this term spirituality means? There seems to be multiple views of spirituality. One view sees spirituality as tied to one's religious affiliation. Another view defines spirituality as something originating from the inside of the individual. Another perspective argues that spirituality involves existentialist questions such as "what is the meaning of my work" and "why I am doing this work?" It is a feeling of being connected with one's complete self, others and the entire universe.

"Spiritual Passion is the dynamic force enabling you to live your life and soul's purpose through the connection of your intellectual, emotional spiritual and physical being".

Father Trudged, a Benedictine Monk, notes that the word spirituality drives from the Latin verb "Spirare" to breathe and the noun spirituals, a breath, so it involves ideas of energy or a force behind life. He further added that spirituality involves-growth- about becoming a person in the fullest sense. It involves relationships, a kind of spiritual hospitality towards others' emotions, honesty, self-belief, behaviour and practices.

The multiple definitions of the meaning of spirituality are natural and logical due to the very personal nature of the word. Following is the representative list of some of the many definitional attempts to date:

Definition of spirituality	*Source*
(1) Spirituality is a principle that originates from the inside of an individual or our inner consciousness.	Guillory (2000 pp. 33) Intrinsic Origin View
(2) The animated force that inspires one towards purposes that are beyond one's self and that gives one's life meaning and direction.	McKnight 1984 (142)
(3) Spirituality involves ultimate and personal truth.	Wong 1998 (354)
(4) Spirituality is doing the work with utmost devotion. Its efforts towards the goal are most important, results are supposed to be provided by god.	The Bhagvad Gita (Karmanyevadhik aarasthe)
(5) The search for meaning in what we are doing at the workplace.	Naylor etc. Al 1996, Neck and Milli Man 1994
(6) It is the desire to find ultimate purpose in life and to live accordingly.	Gerald Cavanagh

Fig. 1

Broadly speaking, spirituality encompasses the ultimate ends of life- the questions of "meaning and purpose of life". The underlying assumption is that everyone and everything has a purpose. Spirituality assumes that there is more to life than our material self and existence. As one writer puts it "We are not human beings on a spiritual journey, we are spiritual beings on a human journey.

Spirituality at the Workplace – An emerging Paradigm

"Defining spirituality in the workplace is like capturing an angel. Explaining workplace spirituality is ethereal and beautiful but perplexing."

"Spirituality at the workplace" is expressed in many ways. Its definition and application are unique to individuals. There are many possible ways to understand such a complex and diverse term. Thompson (2001) denotes that spirituality at the workplace has to do with how you feel about your work, whether it is a job or a calling. Sanders *et al.* (2004) define spirituality at the workplace as the extent to which the organisation encourages a sense of meaning and interconnectedness among their employees. Sheep (2004) defines this term through four components - self workplace integration, meaning in work, transcendence of self and personal growth of one's inner life at work. Viewing the fundamental conceptualisation of spirituality and definitions given in contemporary literature indicates that spirituality is a multi-dimensional, multi-level phenomenon. It includes the practice of humanistic and employee-friendly work environment, service orientation, creativity and innovation, personal and collective transformation, honesty, trust and patience. The key elements in integrating spirituality into the workplace are: people service, organisational self awareness, wisdom and new leadership.

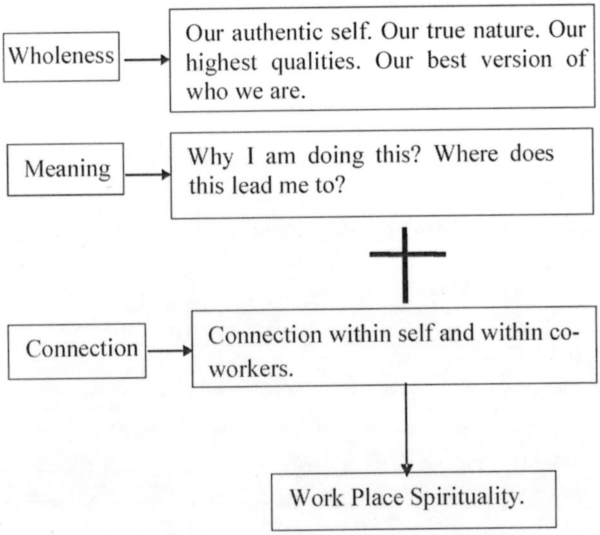

Fig. 2

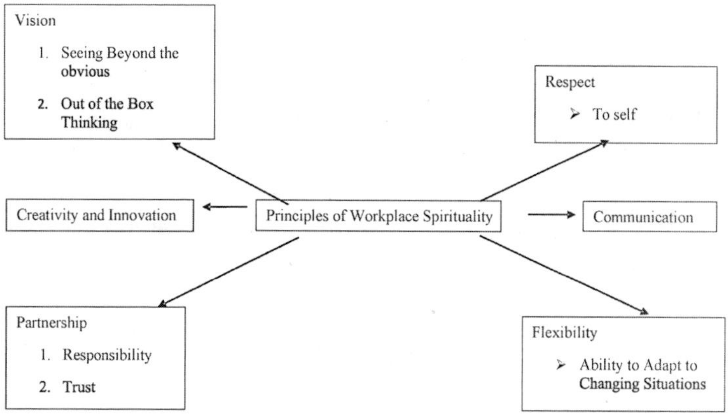

Fig. 3

Reasons for the Call for a Spiritual Workplace

"Organisations, which have long been viewed as rational systems are considering making room for the spiritual dimension, a dimension that has less to do with rules and orders and more with meaning purpose and a sense of community."

Today's workers are no longer willing to work in an authoritarian and dehumanising environment. They want meaning in their work and balance in their lives. Employees want a work place where they both survive and are fully alive. They believe that integrating spirituality in the workplace will allow them to find the meaning and purpose in life. Barrett (n.d.) argued:

"Successful business leaders of 21st century will need to find a dynamic balance between the interest of the corporation, interest of the employees and the interest of society as a whole. (p. 1)." This can be achieved only when organisations link the company's goals of profits with the employees' goal of finding meaning and purpose in their work. Once these are achieved the optimal performance follows.

Individual Level	Group Level
Meaningful work	**Sense of Community**
➢ Enjoy work	➢ Employees support each other
➢ Energized by work	➢ Sense of connection with co - workers
➢ Work give personal meaning and purpose	

Fig. 4

Research suggests that the encouragement of spirituality in the workplace can lead to benefits in the areas of creativity, increased ethical and moral behaviour, personal fulfillment, honesty, trust and commitment which will ultimately lead to increased organisational performance. A survey conducted by East (2005) found that employees who feel spiritually connected at work experience peace of mind, inner strength, patience, calmness, sanity, and a positive attitude. It works both at individual and group level.

1. *Creativity:* "People at all levels in the corporate hierarchy increasingly want to nourish their spirit and creativity" (Corine McLaughlin, 2005). When employees are encouraged to express their creativity, the result is a more fulfilled and sustained workforce. Happy people work harder and are more likely to stay at their jobs.

   "People, who are happy at home and happy at work, are more productive at workplace" - Raizel Robiono.

2. *Honesty:* Another benefit of spirituality is increased authenticity in communication. When the truth is allowed to be safely and respectfully spoken, old problems clear up, new possibilities emerge and people feel more aligned. They work together in a trusting team. Vermont Country Store US, a popular National Catalogue company, honoured instead of fired an

employee who told the truth in a widely circulated memo. This greatly increased morale and built a sense of trust in the company. Honesty is well encouraged within a spiritually enriched company. An honest person is always truthful and trusted by all those who come in contact with. Honesty has a reinforcing effect on patience, integrity reliability, loyalty, forgiveness fearlessness, humility etc. The concept of *"Sathyameva Jayathe"* (As per Hindu Mythology) means, the truth and only truth shall be victorious in the end is one of the most quoted philosophies:

"The only way to achieve success is to express yourself truly in service to society" – *Aristotle.*

3. *Increased ethical and moral behaviour:* It is yet another benefit; an ethical behaviour for a business is the development of trust. We trust people who operate in an ethical framework. In times of economic depression, when the company is not doing well, trust between the management and the employee plays a pivotal role in the future performance of the organisation.
4. *Personal fulfillment and commitment:* Fostering spirituality will lead to employees feeling complete when they come to work. This will result in a high degree of personal fulfillment and increased morals. Spirituality increases commitment by establishing a trustful climate in the workplace. This includes commitment of the employees to the organisation and commitment of the organisation towards employees and customers. In totality, it would lead to an increased organisational performance through greater financial success.

From the above it is obvious that the performance of the organisation and financial success can lean heavily on spiritual enrichment of the workplace. Spirituality is recognised as one of the crucial dimensions of the human personality therefore if an organisation is encouraging spirituality, it is actually encouraging the people to bring their whole self to work (Neck and Millman, 1994) this would mean a greater personal fulfillment and satisfaction and greater commitment to the work and also the organisation. Spirituality is indeed a valuable and inevitable task for the people and when companies will use this tool, they will see the following changes at workplace.

- There will be shift from fear-based culture to love-based culture.
- Organisation will become purpose driven and meaning- based.
- Management practices and decisions will be clearly consistent with spiritual values such as integrity, humility, love, hope, kindness, respect etc.
- Management will learn to truly listen and build a safe place where employees can speak the truth without fear of repercussions.
- Management will break down the walls of hierarchy to create a sense of community and belonging in the workers.
- Employees will be treated in a responsible, respectful and caring ways because people are not instruments to be used and exploited.
- There will be a move from command and control leadership to horizontal servant leadership which emphasises empowering delegation and co-operation.
- There will be an improvement in morale, job satisfaction, loyalty and productivity.

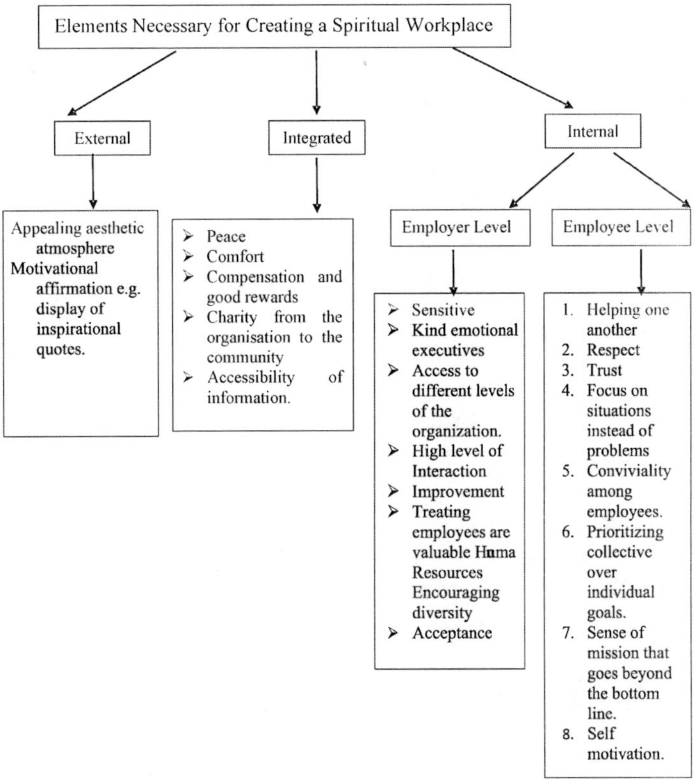
Elements Necessary for Creating a Spiritual Workplace
External
Integrated
Internal
Appealing aesthetic atmosphere
Motivational affirmation e.g. display of inspirational quotes.
Peace
Comfort
Compensation and good rewards
Charity from the organisation to the community
Accessibility of information.
Employer Level
Employee Level
Sensitive
Kind emotional executives
Access to different levels of the organization.
High level of Interaction
Improvement
Treating employees are valuable Huma Resources Encouraging diversity
Acceptance
1. Helping one another
2. Respect
3. Trust
4. Focus on situations instead of problems
5. Conviviality among employees.
6. Prioritizing collective over individual goals.
7. Sense of mission that goes beyond the bottom line.
8. Self motivation.

Fig. 5

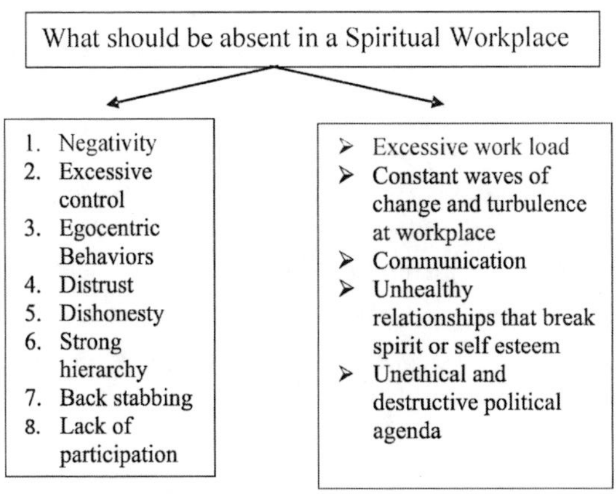
What should be absent in a Spiritual Workplace
1. Negativity
2. Excessive control
3. Egocentric Behaviors
4. Distrust
5. Dishonesty
6. Strong hierarchy
7. Back stabbing
8. Lack of participation
Excessive work load
Constant waves of change and turbulence at workplace
Communication
Unhealthy relationships that break spirit or self esteem
Unethical and destructive political agenda

Fig. 6

Tips to be Spiritually Passionate in the Workplace

Following are a few suggestion/tips to leaders as well as employees to be spiritual passionate at the workplace:

1. *Respect yourself and others:* Respecting yourself and others regardless of age, gender, status, occupational background adds to daily confidence and peace of mind. Respect is a core element of engaging the power of mind, emotional spirit and physical being to move forward with positive action in workplace and life.

2. *Be compassionate to others:* Make the effort to say and do things that take other's views into consideration. Nurture the strengths and success of others. Recognise that we are spiritual beings living as humans who learn from every experience, giving each other a hand up and not a "handout" with our clients and all areas of our life. Being kind and supportive includes teaching, coaching and mentoring others to learn skills in the work that will help them immediately and throughout their career.

3. *Forgiveness:* In organisations where you know that if you make a mistake you're going to be fired there is a culture of fear that stifles productivity. Those who can tolerate mistakes, who see them as learning opportunities, are those who create a great corporate culture. Offer people in your team the chance to take risks, to be creative, to learn and to grow on their own by accepting their mistakes.

4. *Congruence:* Happiness is when what you think, what you say and what you do are in harmony. One of the best tips for being spiritual at the workplace is to behave in a congruent manner and communicate in an authentic way. People seem to really like authentic communication and there is much inner employment to be found when your thoughts words and actions are aligned.

5. *Trust your intuition and wisdom:* Intuitive guidance is the only reliably tool to make you know and realise what is good and what is bad. It is a definite reality and there is

profound wisdom in listening to it. Do not fight intuition have the courage to listen to it and act accordingly.

6. *Be open to change:* "Change begins with the man in the mirror"- *Mahatma Gandhi.*

Change is the only constant factor in life. Challenge yourself to change, to look ahead and move on. If you are willing to alter your beliefs, habits and behaviour you open up new possibilities for fighting your resistance to change.

7. *Wear your attitude:* "The greatest discovery of my generation is that a human being can alter his life by altering his attitude" - *William James.*

William James wrote these words about 100 years ago, and they are just as meaningful today. One of the most over used words in today's society is "attitude". Yet, it remains the most critical element in superior services, successful teamwork, financial outcomes and relationships. Life is all about choices. Your attitude is the personal choice you make about how you react and act in any given situation of your reaction to what happens and your perception of the situation creates your attitude and how you will respond. How you live your life is your choice. Choose to have a great attitude and you will choose a future.

8. *Emotional Control:* "Nobody can hurt me without my permission" - *Mahatma Gandhi.*

What you feel and how you react to something is always up to you. The greatest thing we can recognise is that we are always in control of our response to any situation. We can choose our own thought reactions and emotions to pretty much everything. There is no need to freak out overreact or even react in a negative way if you see something has happened, calm down and think about it. But do not over obsess. If you have harsh standards about what is right and wrong you can have a tendency to go over and over. Always remember that forgiving and letting go of the past will do you and the people in your world a great service.

9. *Persistence:* "A little more persistence, a little more effort and what seems hopeless failure may turn to glorious success"- Eleber Hubbard.

Be persistent, it pays. In times the oppositions around you will face and fall away and your inner resistance and self-sabotaging tendencies that want to hold you back and keep you like you have aim been will grown weaker.

"First they ignore you
Then they laugh at you
Then they fight you
Then you win" - *Mahatma Gandhi*

10. *Remember to say thank you:* Do not take all the credit. Remember to recognise the efforts of others and say thank you at every opportunity. This will enhance team spirit and efforts by letting colleagues know their under backup are acknowledged and appreciated.

"Gratitude opens the door to the power, the wisdom and the creativity you open the door through gratitude" - *Deepak Chopra.*

11. *Trust the process:* Give up the need to have everything planned to the last detail. This is not a realistic approach and can set you up for significant stress in your workplace and life. Certainly plan and identify details at the same time, accept and plan for the unexpected, as this is real life, real work and the real world.

Be confident in your abilities. This is the key to keep up your spirits self-esteem, productivity and healthy relationships. Challenging times, uncertainty and new developments are all part of real work and real life. Strengthening the spiritual passion is a life-long process that will evolve and grow in its own time.

Conclusion

From the above discussion it is clear that the next phase of the evolution of work has begun. Spirituality is becoming more openly recognised as an integral part of the workplace. It has been proved that spirited workplaces have done better with respect to profitability. However, due to the diversity in the beliefs and definitions that each individual has about spirituality, it will be ideal if managers can encourage the employees to follow their own spiritual path and relate that to the goals of the organisation.

References

1. Alfano and Glover Scott, Awakening the Workplace, Dorling Kindersley (India) Pvt. Ltd. Pearson Power, pp. 31-45. 2006
2. Corinne McLaughlin; Spirituality and Ethics in Business; The Centre for Visionary Leadership; 2009.
3. Gauri Chhabra; An eye for an eye, not any more, *Hindustan Times*; HT Career Guide Wednesday October 2, 2013.
4. Gibbons P. Spirituality at Work; A Pre-Theoretical Overview, M.Sc. Dissertation University of London, 2000.
5. Joan Marques, Satinder Dhiman, Richard King "Spirituality in the Workplace: what it is, why it matters; How to make it work for you". Personhood Press Fannskin 2007, (pp. 3-15).
6. Kenneth E. Goodpaster; Work, Spirituality and the Moral Point of View; *International Journal of Value Based Management,* Volume 7, Issue 1, pp. 49-62 1994.
7. Sai A. Vaidyanathan; Bapu's Class Act; The Tribune Jobs and Careers, Wednesday October 2, 2013.
8. Sukmara Kurup Krishna Kumar and Christopher P. Neck, The "What, Why and How of Spirituality in the Workplace"; *Journal of Managerial Psychology,* Volume 17, Number 3, 2002 pp. 153-14.
9. William E. Hala, The New Management. Bringing Democracy and Markets inside Organisations, Berrett BK Koehler 2001.
10. www.martinruthee.com/martinart.html.dt.

6

Integration of Ancient Wisdom with Modern Ethics in Business Scenario

Rashmi Kamra and Gaurav Vij

Introduction

"Business ethics are rules of business conduct by which propriety of business activities may be judged." Biswanath Ghosh in *Ethics in Management and Indian Ethos.*

Business ethical issues are the interaction of economic behaviour with non-economic concerns. The idea of business ethics has attracted the attention of the media, academics and business institutions. Wealth which is acquired with a knowledge of the proper means and without any foul practices will lead to virtue and happiness, as *http://tamils.tamilpower.com* informs us. To supplement that lesson in ethics, the next verse says, "*Wealth gained by loss of love and grace, let man cast off from his embrace.*"

Present Business Scenario

Today the economies across the globe witness a massive shakeout due to the financial turmoil in the US economy. In spite of new upcomings of innovative business models and best practices, there are incidents of corporate scams, bankruptcy etc. There is a long list of failed corporate giants as they do not consider the ethical issues while making business transactions and completely disregard the well being of their employees and common shareholders. There is a total lack of moral conscience and the magnitude of their mismanagement is increasing in this race of economic prosperity. This has forced us to take a fresh look at both the current management programmes and prevailing business practices. There is an urgent and alarming need to address these issues to create a morally healthy business environment for sustainable economic growth. These issues are raising doubts about the sustainability of the existing management practices and principles.

The inclusion of ethics on the agenda was prompted by the importance of the issue to the corporate intelligent community, and the belief that ethical lapses by CI practitioners often result from ignorance rather than intent (Sapia-Bosch and Tancer, 1998). Is ethics really a problem in the corporate intelligent community? Empirical research on the subject suggests the answer is unclear. Business ethics professors Trevino and Weaver performed a SCIP-sponsored literature review and study of ethical practices in CI. They found that while some organisations addressed CI ethics "...quite seriously, most CI practitioners felt left on their own, relying on personal background and intuition to make tough ethical decisions" (Trevino and Weaver, 1997). They further concluded that current ethical guidance was too vague to be truly helpful.

When some companies failed miserably, management consultants, experts and senior management executives started giving a lot of economic reasons for the downfall.

But all blame cannot be put to economic reasons only but it could have been wrong management decisions because of greed, lust, exploitation, rivalry, pride or vanity, etc. The fundamental reason for such negative consequences could be their ego which led to false vanity. It is only by anchoring to one's self that the negative effects of ego can be overcome. The modern management thinkers who are not aware of such issues are still wondering as to

1. What could have gone wrong in those companies which failed miserably in the recent past,
2. What could have led to the sub-prime crisis,
3. What could be the reason that a successful company gets embroiled in a corporate scam.

Now there Arises a Question

How India can survive and contribute towards making the existing modern management paradigms more sustainable in the environment of business uncertainty?

The answers to these questions lie within the organisation. Vedic philosophy of business excellence answers the above questions. It gives extensive focus on broadening ethical boundaries. There is need to bridge the gap between public accountability and private morality. History is full of examples to show that structures, systems, civilisations, without ethical and moral content as their foundation, are sooner or later bound to collapse. Efforts are required to integrate the insights drawn from ancient Indian traditions with modern management practices to promote dynamic leadership management and enlightened corporate decisions. Our rich and traditional Indian ethos have stood the test of time and these are 3500 years old. Most of the wisdom from Indian ethos is derived from the ancient scriptures Vedas, Upanishads, Ramayana, Bhagavada Gita, Arthshastra etc. These ancient Indian texts guide modern business practices and principles to develop sustainability and fill the existing gaps in the present framework of modern management practices. These ancient ethics simultaneously emphasise social welfare along with profit motive.

Managing Self and Management-by-Objectives (MBO) vis-a-vis Vedanta

Peter Drucker said that modern management is primarily based on the workers, their knowledge of self and inner strength. The strengths are then transformed into their core competencies which will help them in performing their tasks more efficiently and thus attain the overall organisational success.

However, this tenet of managing self is not new. It relates back to the Vedanta periods. In the Upanishads, it is said:

"Atmaivedam agra asit purusavidhah, so'nuviksya nanyad atmano'pasyat, so'ham asmitygre vyaharat; tato'ham namabhavat, tasmad apy etarhy amantritah; aham ayam ity evagrauktva, athanyan nama prabrute yad asya bhavati. Sa yat purvo'smat sarvasmat sarvanpapmana ausat, tasmat purusah; osati ha vai sa tam, yo'smat purvo bubhusati, ya evamveda..."

-(1.4.1, Brhadaranyaka Upanisad, Radhakrishnan, 1953)

This means that:

"In the beginning, this world was only self in the form of a person or individual. When he looked around himself he saw nothing else than the self. So he said, 'I am'. Therefore arose the name 'I'. Even to this day when one is addressed he says 'This is I' and then speaks whatever other name he may have...."

Further, the concept of self was well elaborated in the Karma Yoga of Bhagavad Gita where Lord Krishna said:

"indriyâni parâny âhur indriyebhyah param manah
manasas tu para buddhir yo buddheh paratas tu sah"

(3.42, The Bhagavadgîtâ)

This means that -

> "The senses are said to be superior to the body, the mind is superior to the senses, and intellect is superior to the mind and that which is superior to the intellect is He (Self, Atman)."

People who do not realise their Self are controlled by their senses instead of their mind or intellect. And hence, their decisions are based on temptation sand they invariably make mistakes. The great Indian mystics age Ramakrishna (who was the 'guru' or master of Swami Vivekananda) said:

> "The world is water and the mind milk. If you pour milk into water they become one; you cannot find the pure milk any more. But turn the milk into curd and churn it into butter. Then, when that butter is placed in water, it will float. So, practice spiritual discipline in solitude and obtain the butter of knowledge and love. Even if you keep that butter in the water of the world the two will not mix. The butter will float. (Swami Nikhilananda, 1977)

Here the world actually signifies the material world. And it is only through spiritual discipline which includes self-restraint from all material temptations that we can really attain the higher Self or Brahman. Swami Parthasarathy, the modern Vedanta guru who is well known for his corporate workshops on Vedanta says:

> 'Do not lose the treasure of your Self for the pleasure of the sense".(www.vedantainstitute.co.in)

Finally, every person has his own dream and personal goals. Sometimes they try to undermine the broader organisational goals in front of their personal goals and this leads to conflict. To remove such conflicts, modern management (Peter Drucker) advocates the concept of "Management by Objectives" (in short, MBO). However, his concept of MBO is misunderstood in practice as managers tend to take a narrow view of this "objective" where it only covers achievement on individual level instead of achieving the broader organisational goals. To really make MBO instrumental in any organisation, it is important that managers understand their "Karma" in its entirety. The concept of Karma comes from the "Karma-Yoga" of Bhagavad Gita in which Lord Krishna says to Arjuna:

> *"Karmanye Vadhikaraste Ma Phaleshu Kadachana*
> *Ma Karma Phala Hetur Bhurma tey Sangostva Akarmani"*

(2.47, The Bhagavadgîtâ)

It means that "we have only the right to work, right on our actions but not on the consequences or fruits of that action. So we should be not be attached to either fruits of the action or inaction. And then Lord Krishna subsequently said:

> *"Doorena hy Avaram karma, Buddhi-Yogaad Dhananjaya*
> *Buddhau Saranam anviccha, Kripanaah phala-hetavah"*

(3.49, The Bhagavadgîtâ)

This means that we should not work for results, rather we should work with an ideal (Buddhi-Yoga) or a vision because if we work for results, then our work will culminate once we achieve the result. However, when we work with an ideal or vision and we keep on striving to reach it so that in the process of delivering our Karma we grow. Hence, work with an ideal, a vision is far more superior to work for results. So in the context of modern management, every manager should focus on his work and at the same time be "in-sync" with the organisation's vision. When every worker and manager will focus on the Organisation's Vision and mission, then it ultimately leads to excellence. This is the true essence of management by objectives as preached by Drucker. Finally, in the words of Drucker:

> "Workmanship is essential—an organisation demoralises if it does not demand of its members the highest workmanship they are capable of. But there is

always a danger that the true workman, the true professional, will believe that he is accomplishing something when, in effect, he is just polishing stones or collecting footnotes. Workmanship must been courage in the business enterprise. But it must always be related to the needs of the whole."

(Drucker, 1974)

Drucker's "workmanship" actually refers to the "Karma" in the verse 47 and 49 of Bhagavada Gita. When Drucker said that "it must always be related to the needs of the whole" he actually meant work with ideals and work which is in-sync with the organisation's mission. His notion of workmanship is also consistent with the Gita's teaching that the result of work should not be an end in itself.

Need to Revisit the Drucker's Management Principles

Drucker maintains a simultaneous emphasis on Profit as well as welfare. He said –

"It is not enough to do well; it must also do good. But in order to 'do good,' a business must first 'do well."

(Pearce et al., 2010)

Clearly, the concept of Management by Objectives is consistent with the teachings of Bhagavad Gita and ancient Indian wisdoms. However, MBO, Managing Self or workmanship is not possible without workers' consistent pursuit of knowledge creation and acquisition that gradually aligns his individual goals with the broader mission and vision of the enterprise. And that really is instrumental in achieving the goal of MBO as well as managing Self. It is through *jnana srsti* and *jnana prapti* that the individual achieves the motive of attaching his Atman to Brahman in an organisational framework which provides him/her with the motivation to constantly strive for excellence on the path of Karma.

The journey from the level of Self-Management to Creation of a Uniform World order is through creation of knowledge, exchange and transfer of knowledge at various levels. It is this knowledge which relates the individual to the universal order. This concept really goes with the Vedanta school of thought where the ultimate aim of any person is to connect his "Atman" "Individual Self" with the "Brahman" (Universal Self).

The Six-fold path towards for connecting self with universe is through Knowledge or "Jnana". The Six-Fold path of knowledge and levels of management has the following steps:

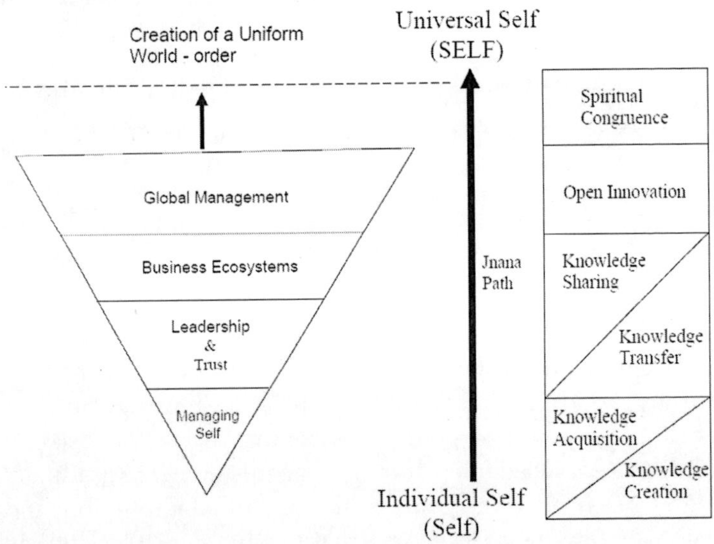

Fig. 1: Connecting Self with Universe.

Kautilya's Arthshastra

The roots of good governance can be traced back in ancient Indian scriptures. There are many universal truths contained in the Arthshastra which can be useful in the study of the modern science of business management. The need of the time is to revive them. Kautilya's Arthshastra gives a full process for the king to take decisions after consulting his ministers, officials and public where required. He discussed participative leadership in fourth century BC. His thoughts are

1. Discuss with ministers and employees.
2. Obtain consultation from people outside the ministry.
3. Encourage constructive confrontation and hear the opinions of all.
4. Selection of advisers should not be on random basis, the qualification and knowledge of advisers is a prerequisite.
5. Opinions of competitors should be sought along with those from friends.
6. In the normal course of business the king should discuss with three-four ministers.
7. Last, but not least, Kautilya defines that the king should choose to hold a collective meeting or individual interactions depending on the situation.

Kautiliya has comprehensively covered most of the aspects of participative leadership in his Arthshastra. With globalisation and the increasing magnitude and complexity of business, participative leadership is gaining importance. He said, a King (a leader) should be *Rajarishi*" which means a king (a leader) who is wise like a sage. Like a sage, a leader must have self-control, conquered his senses and at the same time he should be well-educated in the various fields of knowledge. Successful organisations with revered corporate leaders can follow this wisdom of *Arthashastra*, as the Rajarshi paradigm clearly advocates a leadership which is both responsible and ethical. The process of *jnana parivahana* (knowledge transfer) and *jnana sahabhâjana* (knowledge sharing) can be instrumental in making this *Rajarshi* paradigm a reality in today's corporate leadership. Modern leadership can be in tune with with *Rajarshi* paradigm in the following ways:

(1) *Jnana parivahana* through continuous and intensive training and development programmes for the various levels of managers.

(2) Implementing proper ERP models for knowledge sharing (*jnana sahabhâjana*) so as to enable managers to take effective decisions.

(3) Mentorship of the newly appointed management trainees.

(4) Continuous acknowledgement of the performance of the various employees and managers.

(5) Creating effective management development programmes for the emergence of responsible leadership at different levels of management.

(6) Creating an ethical code of conduct which should promote ethics and transparency.

(7) Enact stringent policy measures to counter any possible unethical practice at various levels 'Chankya Niti', moves a step further and emphasises that even at the cost of loss to the organisation, the larger and common interest of society should prevail in decision-making. Only by managing self and acknowledging the interconnectedness through knowledge transfer and knowledge sharing, sustainable paradigm can be created as the following hymn says:

"One should sacrifice the individual interest for the sake of family, family for the sake of village, village for the sake of nation, and abandon everything for defending higher values of life".

Sacrifice for the larger interest of the society will lead to complete transformation of the corporate world and will provide better society at large which will lead to a new world order.

Buddhism vis-a-vis Leadership

The eightfold path of Gautama Buddha clearly depicts the qualities of a great leader along the path of Knowledge

1.	Right View	Wisdom
2.	Right Intention	
3.	Right Speech	Ethical Conduct
4.	Right Action	
5.	Right Livelihood	
6.	Right Effort	Moral Development
7.	Right Mindfulness	
8.	Right Concentration	

Fig. 2: The Eight Fold Path (Source:thebigview.com)

So, wisdom, moral conduct and intellectual development are the broad themes on which any leader should work upon. Meditation or Yoga is of great importance for gaining control of the five senses and develop the level of concentration and is becoming so popular across the globe.

Upanishads

The Upanishads deal with the philosophical questions: What is the nature of the ultimate reality? What is the essence of the humanity? The essence of humanity and the essence of the world, the ancient philosophers produced the greatest insight of the Upanishads. The Upanishads also give the doctrine of Karma. According to their thought, each human soul lives countless lives. It is born and reborn again and again until it reaches liberation and is born no more. In life, the individual suffers and enjoys the results of immoral or moral deeds done in existing and previous lives. In turn, the individual performs deeds whose fruits he will reap in existing and succeeding lives. Every moral act must lead to its appropriate reward: if not in this life, then in a future one. In the same way in an organisation, perceptions of customers, employees, shareholders, suppliers and society about the concern are based on its past performance and current deeds. Also, the positive initiative taken by the organisation will definitely fetch good rewards now or in the future. Therefore, an organisation should continuously focus on improvements. This is how the business practices throughout the world are correlated with the similar inferences already existing in Vedic literature.

Essence of Business Excellence vis-a-vis Vedic Vision

Man has been striving for excellence. Excellence in all deeds is the simplest way to attain God. It implies competence and striving for highest possible standards. The dictionary meaning of excellence is "Quality of highest order". Business excellence models adopted by various countries are dynamic in nature and periodically go under review for further improvements based on the changing needs of stakeholders. They reflect shifts in business emphasis and new management approaches and ideas. They can be used by any organisation irrespective of country, size, sector or maturity in excellence. These concepts have very deep linkage with the Vedic concept of business excellence. Business is a legitimate and integral part of society. It creates wealth for society through manufacturing, distribution, foreign trade, financing and other activities. Business works for "Sarva Lok Hitam" which means "the well-being of all stakeholders". As per Indian mythology, "Swa-Dharma" or "Self-Ethics" or "Organisation's Values System" are synonyms for quality. To attain the excellence or "quality of highest order" everyone in an organisation needs to perform his duty whole heartedly and correctly and completely without any deviation from the standard. Excellence is dependent upon balancing and satisfying the needs of all relevant stakeholders including employees, customers, suppliers, shareholders and society in general. It is in line with the following Vedic hymn:

"Effort is the hallmark of a human being".

Quality

Quality is the ability of a product or service to consistently meet or exceed customer expectations. Quality has many dimensions, for example, performance, aesthetics, conformance, safety, reliability, durability, after sale service etc. Quality means meeting or exceeding expectations. According to Indian mythology, there are sixteen dimensions of quality. If a man could attain the excellence even in one dimension or aspect of life, he becomes entitled to salvation or Moksha. It is believed that Lord Rama attained the excellence in fourteen dimensions (fourteen Kala Sampuran) and Lord Krishna attained the excellence in sixteen dimensions (sixteen Kala Sampuran).

Constancy of Purpose and Continuous Improvement Focus

The focus should be on creation of the aim and purpose of the organisation and then the concentration should be upon policy and strategy of the company to understand the basic purpose of its creation. Rig-Veda explains the "Rta", or "cosmic order", which means that physical as well as moral laws govern the entire universe and that no transgression of the laws is allowed. The following mantra from Rig-Veda clearly explains this concept:

"O ye mankind!

Let your vision and thinking of life be one and common,

Let your hearts be transpired with feeling of equality,

Let your minds be united together,

Resulting in equal prosperity and common excellence in the Life for all".

The concept of continuous learning, innovation and improvement of excellence models emphasise the same thing. The emphasis on continuous efforts for improvements to attain excellence is supported by Vedic hymn:

"The Gods like hard-working persons. They dislike easy-going and idle people. Ever-wakeful persons attain great happiness and prosperity".

Another Vedic hymn focuses on continuous improvements:

"O man! You grow very high".

Customer Satisfaction

The customer is the real king of the business. Customer loyalty, retention, and market share gain are best optimised through clear focus on the needs of current and prospective customers. Management must know their responsibilities and give priority to customer satisfaction. Customer satisfaction can be achieved through "Self-Inspection" or "Organisation's Values System", which will lead to achievement of excellence (Yoga) of product or service.

Leadership

In the Bhagavad Gita, Krishna advises Arjuna that 'enlightened leaders should master any impulses or emotions that cloud sound judgment.'

The policy of an organisation's leaders creates a clarity and unity of purpose within the organisation and builds a congenial and competitive environment. All business excellence models put leadership as the first step towards excellence. Manu Smiriti has many mantras, which guides how good governance can be achieved. Role model ethics by the chief executive plays a major role in the development of organisational culture. Employees will follow the "Swa-Dharma" or Organisation's Values System only if the chief executive and his team sets an example before them. Vedic philosophy explains:

"As the chief executive (King) is, so are the people".

The eminent international quality experts like Deming, Claus Moller and Harry Roberts also endorse the same principle and deliberately identify the personal quality of the chief executive as the pivot point for organisational excellence. The search of personal quality starts from self-analysis. Vedic shastras strongly pointed the need of three types of self-discipline to be strictly observed by the Shreshtha Purusha (man with high moral ethics) or the chief executive of an organisation.

- Atma-Glanior: Self-Guilt,
- Ishwar-Bhayao: Fear of punishment by God, and
- Lok-Lajjaor: Fear of Society.

Employee Development

The potential of an organisation's employees is best released through shared values and a culture of trust and empowerment. Each employee must be oriented to the organisation's philosophy of commitment to never-ending improvement through education, training and self-improvement. Management should drive out fear and create an environment of trust and innovation so that everyone may effectively contribute. The hymn of Atharva Veda endorses the above concept:

> "O King! Take care of the welfare and growth of all your people. Then you will grow as the sun grows and shine sat dawn and after the sun makes consistent and continuous efforts to grow without fear."

Similarly, the chief executive should make continuous efforts for the growth of his employees and the organisation. The quality of a person's life is directly proportional to his commitment to excellence.

Partnership Focus

An organisation which has mutually beneficial relationships, built on trust, sharing of knowledge, and integration with its partners will work more effectively. Instead of minimising total cost, there should be a move toward a single supplier for any one item and build the long-term relationship of loyalty and trust. The improvement in organisational performance, practices, and capabilities is possible only through teamwork, sharing of best practice information among organisations. Benchmarking offers the sharing of experiences with peers from other institutions in a friendly atmosphere. Participation in benchmarking clubs by a variety of companies makes it easy to find companies that have different strengths. Thus, the team spirit among the organisations play a major role in high growth, as the hymn in 'Atharva Veda' says,

"People with same divine thoughts grow together".

Focus on enablers (actions) to achieve results is truly in line the hymn from Bhagavad Gita:

"Don't be associated with inaction".

The scriptures moved a step further and stressed continuous efforts with detachment. A hymn from 'Yajur-Veda' says,

"One should like to live in this world doing hard work for 100 years. There is no other way for one's salvation. A selfless and detached action keeps the doer away from harm". The selfless actions will lead one to the highest level of happiness (Moksha).

Distribution of Wealth for Growth

According to Vedic philosophy, one should continuously distribute one's wealth for growth. The moment one stops the distribution, the rate of growth starts declining. The 'Atharva Veda' has a sutra to explain this aspect:

> "O man! Procure wealth with 100 hands and distribute it in charity with 1,000 hands. Thus, you attain perfection of the work done and to be done".

New organisations and areas of business sprout up with the distribution of wealth and provide new opportunities for growth. Thus, the organisations should continuously search for new opportunities for business and capital investment with an objective of growth for all. While it will generate more employment avenues and better prosperity for the society, it will also give an opportunity for the development of the employees, suppliers, and customers and ultimately lead to more profits.

Yoga—Path of Excellence

According to Patanjali: "Yoga is a methodical effort to attain excellence".

It is achieved through the control of the different elements of human nature. All states of mind are modifications of "chitta" (mind). Ordinary human life is afflicted by egoism, attachment to pleasure, aversion to pain, and love of life and these are responsible for the greatest turbulence in "chitta". In the state of "samadhi", all modifications of "chitta" cease, and the soul regains its eternal and attains a perfect state (or excellence). It becomes free, self-illuminated consciousness as Patanjali says:

"Ending the functions of chitta is Yoga".

In an organisation there are clashes of interests among various stakeholders for their conflicting demands leading to day to day problems and fire fighting by one and all. By ceasing all these afflictions an organisation can become excellent or ideal. At this stage every member of the organisation works not because he will be rewarded but because it gives him inherent happiness. It is the stage of self-actualisation.

"You have right to perform your karma (action), but never to the fruits thereof. Never consider yourself the cause of the results of your activities, nor should you be attached to inaction".

To attain this level of thinking in one's thoughts, we need to have the selflessness in ourselves and in the organisations.

Spiritual Congruence - Creating a Uniform World Order

True globalisation would be about embracing every culture and facilitating a healthy acculturation process. Outsourcing, strategic partnerships, off-shoring etc. make the world into one global village. For making globalisation more inclusive and facilitating a positive acculturation process "spiritual congruence" should be taken along. Earlier, organisations have tried to approach new cultures either in "Superiority" approach (that our products, values, cultures, etc. could be superior to the host country's culture, products, values, etc.) or in "Pragmatic" approach (that our products and offerings are more suitable to their needs and as per their tastes and preferences and along with it we respect their culture).

However, both these approaches somehow fail to bring complete "harmony" between the two cultures, two nations. So, a third way is recommended which is called the "commonality" approach based on Spiritual congruence. Any culture comprises some fundamental values based upon religion. Spiritual congruence is an ideal step in this perspective. Instead of identifying individual differences, it is about finding the commonalities between the various religions. Every religion has certain common views and perspectives on certain important virtues of humanity like righteousness, humility, peace, trust, brotherhood, knowledge, ego, etc. Institutions will have to play a leading role towards facilitating this process of spiritual congruence to create a global environment. Healthy trade relations based on a feeling of oneness could certainly go a long way and can be traced back to the most ancient Indian scripture, the Rig Veda which contained the most important idea of commonality –

"Ekam satya viprah bahudha vadanti"

(The Rig Veda, Book I, Hymn CLXIV, Verse 46)

Which means that truth is one but sages call it by various names.

The answer to the process of Spiritual congruence could be attained from the Upanishad which says:

"Yasmin sarvai bhutany atmaivabhud vijnatah
Tatra ko mohah kah sokah ekatvam anupasyate"

(Isa Upanishad, 1.7)

Which means that whoever sees all beings in Self and the Self in all beings, hates none. In an organisational context, the idea of oneness and spiritual congruence should be emphasised to have an ethical organisational culture based on virtues of truthfulness (transparency), trust (employer-employee, employee-employee and employee-stakeholder), righteousness (justice, equity and honesty), sense of cooperation, etc.

Swami Vivekananda said a century ago.

"This grand preaching, the oneness of things, making us one with everything that exists, is the great lesson to learn."

Conclusion

In essence, the Veda are answers to many questions. This can be achieved through integrating efforts to maximise the global product and its equitable distribution among members of society. In the new millennium, it will be essential for the business leaders to devise and adopt a unified theory focused to attain excellence. Business practices will have to be changed and aligned to with the growing needs and expectations of stakeholders. To bring excellence, the integration of the Vedic studies with modern science and technological research is necessary.

Finally, following verse from the Kena Upanishad supports this:

Pratibodha-viditam matam amrtatvam hi vindate
Atmana vindate viryam vidyaya vindate amrtam.

(Kena Upanishad, 2.4)

"When it is known through every state of cognition, it is rightly known, for by such knowledge one attains life eternal; through one's own self one gains power and through wisdom one gains immortality". So, modern management is toothless without ancient Indian wisdom. It is only when we integrate the ancient Indian wisdom into the modern management that we will transcend this current stage of crisis and emerge in a more enlightened and sustainable form. It is time that modern management thinkers should emphasise the importance of ancient Indian ethos and fill the gaps that exist in the existing paradigms of leadership and management to create the new world order. In words of Jalaluddin Rumi –

> "Don't be satisfied with stories, how things have gone with others. Unfold your own truth."

References

Atharva Veda 20-18-3, 4-4-2, 3-24-5.

Aurobindo, Sr. (1956), The Secret of the Veda, Sri Aurobindo Ashram Publication.

Aurobindo, Sr. (1971), The Upanishads, Sri Aurobindo Ashram Publication.

Bhawuk Dharam P.S.: 2011, Spirituality and Indian Psychology: Lessons from the Bhagavad-Gita (Springer).

Drucker, P.: 1974, Management: Task, Responsibilities, Practices, *Harper and Row.*

Krishna, P. (2010), Presentation at the National Conference on 'Spirituality and Ethics inManagement' held on 30-31st October 2010 at School of Management Sciences, Varanasi.

Nikhilananda,Swami. 1977, The gospel of Sri Ramakrishna (Ramakrishna-Vivekananda Center) - (Pearce et al., 2010).

Radhakrishnan, S. (1953), The Principal Upanishads, Harper Collins Publishers.

Radhakrishnan, S. (1948), The Bhagavadgita, Harper Bros. Publishers.

Rangarajan, L. (1987), Kautilya's The Arthashastra, Penguin Books Rig Veda, 10-191-4, 8-2-18, 10-191.

Radhakrishnan S.: (1993), The Bhagavada Gita, Harper Collins Publishers.

Sharma, AK, Business excellence enshrined in Vedic Philosophy. Karma Capitalism, Business WeekSapia-Bosch, A, and R. Tancer (1998). "Navigating Through the Legal/Ethical Gray Zone," Competitive Intelligence Magazine, 1(1), 31-36. Shreemad Bhagvad Geeta, Chapter 2 (47), (50).

Sharma, L.N. and Sharma, Sushmita, Kautilya's Indicators of Good Governance, IJPA, op. cit, p. 268.

Singh, S. (2011), Spirituality and the Role of Ego: Insights for Management, Purushartha, 4(1), 1-2.

Trevino, L.K. and G.R. Weaver (1997). "Ethical Issues in Competitive Intelligence Practice: Consensus, Conflicts, and Challenges," Competitive Intelligence Review, 8(1), 61-72.

The CII-EXIM Bank Award for Business Excellence 2002—Application Brochure and The Business Excellence Model, Confederation of Indian Industries Publications, TQM Division, New Delhi.

Vivekananda,Swami. 1901, The Vedanta Philosophy: An Address before the Graduate Philosophical Society at Harvard University on March 25, 1896. The Vedanta Society, New York.

Websiteswww.businessexcellenceaustralia.com.au www.quality.nist.gov

www.vedantainstitute.co.in

www.knowledgeatwharton.com

www.tamils.tamilpower.com

7

Business Ethics and Gender Discrimination in Indian Industry

Shivani Setia and Ritu Kalra

Learned men see with an equal eye
a scholarly and dignified priest,
a cow, an elephant, a dog,
and even an outcaste scavenger.

Introduction

Discrimination is the detrimental treatment of an individual based on their membership of a certain group or category. It involves excluding or restricting members of one group from opportunities that are available to another group. Discriminatory behaviour takes many forms, but they all involve some form of exclusion or rejection. Gender discrimination in the workplace happens when an employee is treated differently because of his or her gender. Whenever gender discrimination in the workplace adversely affects the terms and conditions of employment, it is against the law.

The focus of this chapter is on issues concerning gender disparities in the context of Indian Industry so as to examine the nature of prevalent discrimination and biases against women. Gender discrimination in economic activities is a matter of concern for any democratic and developing country. Equal opportunity and compensation to female workforce are required to be in-built in the government policies of the country. Gender equality is also enshrined as an international human rights. Most countries now have legislation on equal rights for women and men in the workplace, covering wages, conditions, representation, and promotion, plus fair access to livelihoods and resources.

Everyone, without any discrimination, has the right to equal pay for equal work. However, even in industrialised countries there are large differences in salaries by gender, even within the same occupations. On top of that, there are promotion obstacles for women and women tend to get "sorted" in low-paying professions, sometimes even by the force of law.

Table 1. Work participation rates by gender, 1971 to 2001 (in per cent)

Census (Year)	*T/R/U*	*Female*	*Male*	*Persons*
1971	Total	14.22	52.75	34.17
	Rural	5.92	53.78	35.33
	Urban	7.18	48.88	29.61
1981	Total	19.67	52.62	36.70
	Rural	23.06	53.77	38.79
	Urban	8.31	49.06	29.99
1991	Total	22.27	51.61	37.50
	Rural	26.79	52.58	40.09
	Urban	9.19	48.92	30.16
2001	Total	25.63	51.68	39.10
	Rural	30.79	52.11	41.75
	Urban	11.88	50.60	32.25

Source: Modified from the Report of the Working Group on Empowerment of Women, Planning Commission, Government of India, 2007-2012.

According to the 2001 Census, the work participation rate for women was 25.63 per cent in 2001, which is an improvement from 22.27 per cent in 1991 and 19.67 per cent in 1981. In 2001, the work participation rate for women in rural areas was 30.79 per cent as compared to 11.88 per cent in the urban areas. In the rural areas, women are mainly involved as cultivators and agricultural labourers. In the urban areas, almost 80 per cent of women workers are working in the unorganised sectors like household industries, petty trades and services, buildings and construction.

Although the census figures show a negligible but steady increase in work participation rate for women, the NSSO figures provide a more complex picture. It indicates a decline in work participation rates for women between 1993-94 and 1999-2000 from 28.6 per cent to 25.9 per cent. There was an increase again in 2004-05 to 28.7 per cent, and in recent years there has been a marginal but steady increase in work participation.

Despite rapid economic growth during the last two decades, gender disparities remain deep and persistent in India. The UN Gender Inequality Index ranks India below several Sub-Saharan African countries, and the World Economic Forum ranks India 113 out of 135 countries in its Global Gap Report.

'Gender equality is smart economics ... [it] can have large impacts on productivity. Women now represent more than 40 per cent of the global labour force, 43 per cent of the agricultural workforce, and more than half of the world's university students. For an economy to be functioning at its potential, women's skills and talents should be engaged in activities that make the best use of those abilities.'– 2012 World Development Report, World Bank.

Forms of Gender Discrimination

1. Gender inequality in the workplace can happen in many ways. It may occur during hiring process when men

are hired rather than women with equal skills and experiences. It can be seen in employment benefits such as the number of vacation or training a male or female worker receives.

2. Despite these sexual discriminations within the world of business, both men and women are seeing.
3. A lighter view of gender inequality.
4. ***Discrimination at the work place:*** Women workers are paid differential wages for the same work. They also have limited access to and control over resources, poor access to information and improving skills. Women are often times regarded as additional or supplementary workers, further marginalising their ability to consolidate their position as workers. Aside from this, there is widespread gender bias in recruitment and promotion of women workers.
5. ***Nature of work***: Women are largely found in jobs that are low skilled, labour intensive and repetitive.
6. ***Access to facilities:*** Women have less access to facilities and benefits. Welfare facilities and services such as sanitary facilities, arrangements for drinking, eating and resting, and access to first aid, healthcare and transport are at times not regarded from a gendered perspective. In the case of night work, it is acknowledged that transport and security is provided for women workers.
7. ***Sexual harassment***: Women at the work place are regularly subjected to sexual harassment. Norms to seek redress and remedy through a special procedure for sexual harassment complaints, though mandated by the judgement of the Supreme Court, is rarely found to be implemented.
8. ***Inadequate and poor representation***: Women do not get adequate representation in trade unions, employers' organisations, social dialogue bodies and

other relevant fora so as to address and improve their working conditions.

9. ***Accounting for household work***: Women work both at home and in the labour market. The former (domestic and care work) is rarely given due recognition for the contribution to the labour market.
10. ***More pronounced in India:*** Gender discrimination seems to be more pronounced in India than elsewhere in Asia may reflect the extent to which cultural patterns, and the associated societal pressures on women, are more ingrained here than elsewhere.

Occupational Segregation

Men may be from Mars and women from Venus, but does the difference in gender affect their choice of jobs? Empirically, it would appear so.

At the same time, occupational segregation by sex - the tendency of men and women to work in different occupations - is a common reason for gender differences in wages. Over the years, however, the movement of women into traditionally predominantly male occupations reduced occupational segregation to a considerable degree, as a result of women increasing their representation in previously male white-collar and service jobs significantly faster than the increase in their share of total employment.

In the 1980s and 1990s, for instance, the movement of women into higher-paying, traditionally-male occupations contributed to the narrowing of the gender pay gap. Thus, in 1970, 69 per cent of men worked in heavily-male - defined as 20 per cent or less female - occupations and 45.8 per cent of women were employed in heavily - more than 80 per cent - female occupations. Occupational sex segregation calculations for India also support the fact that a very high proportion of the women (62.2 per cent in 1999-00) are employed in typically female or integrated occupations. However, the decade of 1990s saw a decline of 9-14 per cent in sex segregation levels with significant regional/district level variations. This period coincides with the trade liberalisation phase in India. The factors responsible for the observed fall in gender segregation level include rising levels of educational attainment and human capital of women, increasing presence of feminism, changes in culture and traditions, changes in industrial and occupational structure and perhaps lower levels of gender prejudice on part of the employer, employee or the customer. Though these numbers have become less skewed over the years, occupational segregation persists.

Salaries and Wages

Gender-based wages is one practice in gender inequality. Although many countries have made laws concerning its elimination, some still practice it. This is because of the fact that society still classifies some jobs as women's work or men's work. This is why gender differences concerning salaries can never vanish in every society. Although what is deeply rooted can be hard to uproot, the salary gap can be slowly removed if people will stop believing men are better than women. A gender-neutral atmosphere is an ideal façade for every business establishment.

India has the distinction of being the lowest ranked on gender parity, which includes pay parity, among the BRIC (Brazil, Russia, India, China) economies. This was revealed in the Global Gender Gap Report of 2010. Gender parity in wages has been a global concern for about a century now. Yet progress has been slow after the initial victories.

In India, the Constitution recognised the principle of "Equal Pay for Equal Work" for both men and women, and "Right to Work" through Article 39(d) and 41. As far back as 1976 the Equal Remuneration Act came into effect and yet unequal pay dogs working women in India. From small businesses to large organisations to the unorganised sector, women are paid lesser wages than men for the same work.

According to the Annual Survey of Industries of 2004-05 the gender pay gap for regular workers in the formal or organised sector was 57 per cent, which is much higher than among casual workers in the formal sector which was over 35-37 per cent. And in agriculture, where an estimated 60 per cent of all operations are handled exclusively by women, the hourly wage rates vary from 50 to 75 per cent of male rates.

In case you thought the gender gap is restricted to the lower levels of workers, a survey done by the World Economic Forum (WEF) in 2012 showed that there is a yawning gender gap in the corporate sector, too. The average annual income of a woman is $1,185, less than a third of a man's $3,698 in corporate India.

The survey, based on the responses of 60 of the 100 best employers in India, showed that women employees held only 10 per cent of the senior management positions in two-thirds of the surveyed companies. The government is no better as an employer. Two of its much touted welfare schemes, Integrated Child Development Services (ICDS) and National Rural Health Mission (NRHM) — rely on the underpaid work of lakhs of women who are paid "an honorarium" well below the minimum wage. In the government's bid to keep expenditure low on social schemes it has resorted to the traditionalist view that care work is service rendered by women and even gone to extent of terming these workers "volunteers" so as to avoid paying salary or giving any social security benefits such as pension or health coverage.

Whatever the reason might be for disparity of wages, whether existing social norms and practices or inadequate accounting of the overall work output of women or even women's own diffidence in demanding better pay, the loss women incur from this inequity is estimated to be significantly large. In the US, by not asking for pay parity, a woman employee leaves a whopping million dollars plus on the table over the course of her working life.

Structure of Education and Labour Market in India

The educational levels for the labour force by sex reflect the high proportion of illiterate workers both in rural and urban areas. This continues to be the scenario in spite of the improvements noted over the years. The gap among male and female graduates and above category in urban areas is gradually shrinking. This positive outcome is reflected in direct beneficial increases in women's organised sector jobs even displacing men in these sectors. Except from this minuscule inversion, not much other change seems to be visible.

Table 2: Average Wage/ Salary Earnings (Rs Per Day) Received by Regular Wage/ Salaried Employees of Age 15-59 Years and Female to Male Wage Ratio by Broad Education Category (Rural-Urban), 1999-2000

Education Category	*Rural*			*Urban*		
	Male	*Female*	*F/M ratio*	*Male*	*Female*	*F/M ratio*
Not Literate	71.23	40.32	0.57	87.63	51.83	0.59
Literate and upto middle	91.63	161.48	1.76	105.08	64.41	0.61
Secondary and Higher secondary	148.23	126.09	0.85	168.16	145.73	0.87
Graduate and above	220.93	159.92	0.72	281.55	234.74	0.83
All	127.32	114.01	0.90	169.71	140.26	0.83

Source: NSS (1999-2000)

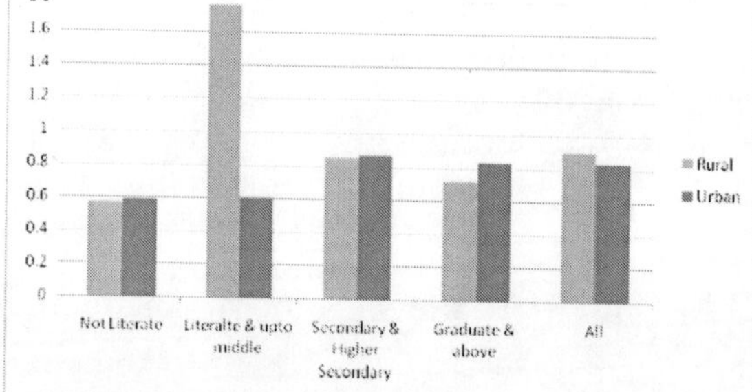

Graph representing Female to Male Wage Ratio by Broad Education Category (Rural-Urban), 1999-2000.

It can be observed from the above table and figure that educational attainment ensures better wages for labourers, both men and women, across educational categories, the average daily wage/salary earnings calculations for regular employees of age 15-59 years display distinct gender wage gap with the wage/earnings of women being lower than that of men across all categories, except for rural women literates up to middle level education.

Occupational health problems of women as seen from a gender perspective

Basically hazards posed by physical, chemical and biological agents in the work place are similar for male and female workers but the following factors have to be remembered for women workers.

Women on an average, have a smaller stature and have less physical strength; their vital capacity is 11 per cent less; their haemoglobin is app. 20 per cent less; their skin area is larger as compared to circulating volume; they have larger body fat content. They have lower heat tolerance and greater cold tolerance.

Woman's unique reproductive function exposes her unborn child to workplace hazards. Women shoulder additional burden of household work, care of children and social responsibilities.

Occupational stress is one of the major problems from a gender perspective. Studies from developed countries show that sources of stress in women's lives are more diverse and diffuse than those experienced by men. A number of factors cause stress among working women. These include:

1. *Multiple overlapping roles:* As housewives, mothers and workers especially when such roles are physically and mentally demanding with little satisfaction, monetary gain or social rewards;
2. *Types of job repetitive and monotonous jobs:* With little control over work pace and methods, piece rate system and job insecurity all lead to stress;

3. *Sexual harassment*: This is often faced by women in almost all types of occupations except when they occupy top level jobs. It is widely believed that employers show a preference for women only when they are prepared to accept lower wages, are expected to be more docile and submissive;
4. *Shift work:* In certain occupations, such as telephone operators who do different shifts including night shifts, interference with family responsibilities causes lot of stress.

Measures by Government

The Indian Constitution guarantees equality to all persons within India; it also prohibits discrimination by the State on the grounds of sex. The equality guarantee is available to all persons within India (not merely citizens), thus extending its scope to all migrants and persons of non-Indian origin in India. Remedies under labour statutes, of course, remain available. For instance, protection against gender-based discrimination in recruitment and promotions is guaranteed by the Equal Remuneration Act, 1976 (ERA).

Women in the unorganised or informal sector are also often not covered under labour laws since these laws are confined to industries/sectors employing a minimum of workers. This is a form of discrimination against unorganised or informal workers. The recently enacted Unorganised Workers'Social Security Act, 2008, aims to provide minimum benefits to such workers.

1. The Sexual Harassment of Women at Workplace (Prevention, Prohibition and Redressal) Act, 2013 is a legislative act in India that seeks to protect women from sexual harassment at their place of work.
2. Workmen Compensation Act.
3. Trade Union Act
4. Payment of Wages Act

5. The Payments of Wages (Procedure) Act, 1937
6. The Minimum Wages Act, 1948
7. The Employees' State Insurance Act, 1948
8. The Factories Act, 1948
9. The Minimum Wages Act, 1950
10. The Contract Labour (Regulation and Abolition) Act, 1970
11. The Equal Remuneration Act, 1976
12. The Bonded Labour System (Abolition) Act, 1979
13. The Inter-State Migrant Workmen (Regulation of Employment and Conditions of Service) Act, 1979.

Inequality and Women's Work Worldwide

Women's experience of work and the sources of their livelihoods vary across the world. However, in all countries women face barriers to equal rights both at work and in the home.

Gender differences in access to land, credit and labour disadvantage women in **China** where firm managers prefer to sign export contracts with men because women have limited access to productive assets, lack statutory rights over land, and have less authority over family (and therefore over potential farm labour).

In Latin America, 50 per cent of women work – a 21 per cent increase in ten years, due in part to a leap in exported goods.

Colombia is the world's second biggest flower exporter, employing 110,000 workers, 65 per cent of them women. During peak times a female worker has to work up to 80 hours a week, earning as little as $1 a day.

In **Kenya**, women own half of all small and medium enterprises, but these experience less growth than male-owned businesses, due to a lack of support and resources.

In sub-Saharan Africa nearly 80 per cent of women workers are in vulnerable employment.

In 14 of the **countries in the EU** group of 28, there is no woman CEO in any of the top 50 publicly quoted companies In the EU, the pay gap increases with age, level of educational attainment, and years of service. For example, it exceeds 30 per cent in the 50–59 age group compared with only 7 per cent for those under 30.

Eastern Europe is the only region where the proportion of women in industry exceeds 20 per cent.

In **Bangladesh**, women make up 80–90 per cent of the textiles industry.

In **Asia**, the Philippines and Thailand both have comparatively high proportions of women among directors and chief executives, with 48 and 32 per cent respectively; the Republic of Korea has the lowest proportion in the region, with just 3 per cent. Averaged over all occupations, women in the Republic of Korea earn 68 per cent of what men earn.

In **India,** at the junior level, women comprise just under 29 per cent of the workforce in these companies in India, which drops off to just under 15 per cent at the middle level, an attrition rate of almost 50 per cent, and to under 10 per cent of the workforce at the senior level.

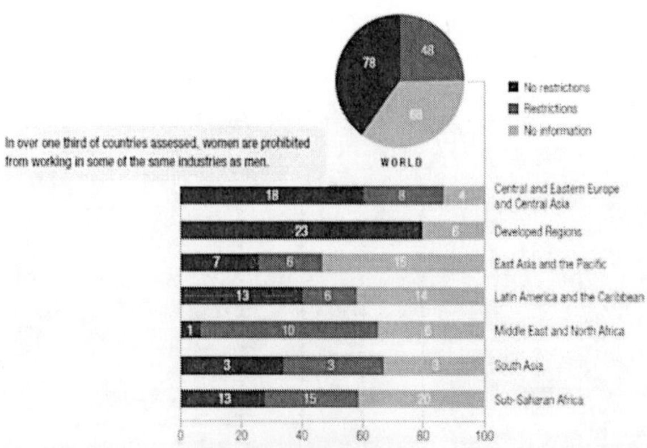

Fig. 1. Legal restrictions on women's right to work.

Source: World Bank 2010f

Note: Based on a World Bank assessment of labour laws using UN Women regional groupings.

Ways to Promote Gender Equality in the Workplace

1. The companies can promote gender inequality by analysing the composition of their board of directors, executive leadership team and staff. Gender equality begins at the highest level of corporate governance to set an example for executives, managers and employees. They can list the areas, groups or occupations where there's an under-representation of women and can then determine how workforce imbalances affect the company. For example, if women are underrepresented in management positions, it deprives the organisation of leadership's diverse talent.
2. Gender inequality can be increased by examining the availability and types of training that offer professional development for all employees, and in particular, experienced and qualified female workers who have been overlooked for promotion to higher level positions. Working women are primarily responsible for coordinating family obligations, child-care arrangements and their job demands. It should implement flexible training options for employees whose schedules prevent them from participating in professional development activities due to scheduling conflicts. One solution is to offer remote access to online training.
3. Every company should review its fair employment practices and policies. It should update policies pertaining to sexual harassment and discrimination based on sex in accordance with Indian Equal Employment Opportunity Commission guidelines and ensures that their organisational policies are congruent with other federal, state and local employment laws.
4. By conducting research on employer policies that accommodate the needs of a diverse, gender-equal work force and exploring various developing and implementing family-friendly initiatives, child-care

options for working parents, educational subsidies and comprehensive benefits packages that meet the needs of traditional and non-traditional family structures.

5. Further, gender inequality can be ensured by developing training for all levels of management and staff on topics such as maintaining gender equity, creating a collegial and collaborative work environment and appreciating diverse talents, skills and capabilities. Encourage individual participation as well as experiential learning through team building exercises and work groups. Establish learning objectives that build upon the foundation of fair employment practices and policies.
6. The companies should design employee opinion surveys and exit interview questions that elicit information about working conditions, employee views about equality, training opportunities and professional development activities. They can develop an action plan template that helps implement changes in response to survey results and can create another template that helps analyse and report the effectiveness of retention strategies.
7. Sign up to the seven Women's Empowerment Principles of UNIFEM and the Global Compact, implement these within your business, and demonstrate through public reporting how a business is living up to them. It should Follow ILO conventions and local laws – whichever give greatest protection to women and men. Take responsibility for understanding how gender discrimination manifests itself in the countries where you operate by talking to trade union bodies, women's groups, and ministries of labour.

Conclusions

The increasing participation levels of women in the paid labour market activities is viewed as a positive outcome for improving women's status by bridging the hiatus in this crucial sphere of economic involvement. However, mere increases in participation remain inadequate in altering the gender inequalities unless these are supported by the nature of work they undertake being decent, lucrative, equally remunerative and secure. If illiterate women are crowding into unskilled, manual labour requiring jobs, that are low paying and hazardous to their health and safety, such a situation can barely be lauded or appreciated.

Government of India has implemented many laws and policies for safety and protection of the female work force, in terms of policies such as The Factories Act, 1948, The Sexual Harassment of Women at Workplace (Prevention, Prohibition and Redressal) Act, 2013, The Equal Remuneration Act, 1976, The Maternity Benefit Act, 1961 etc. for the safety in the work place with specific reference to female workers. However, the gender bias as revealed in the study requires to be removed through proper policy planning and serious institutional corrections.

Therefore, top management must avoid discriminatory practices in hiring, promotion, and facilities to the employees irrespective of what is his/her gender. The human resource managers should be careful while hiring and the promotion of the employees and providing facilities to employees in order to avoid any gender discrimination because it has a direct relationship on employee productivity. The human resource managers should provide facilities and provision of goods according to the ratio of men and women. In the meanwhile promotion of employees should be based on merit and seniority. They must accept the importance of female workers and realise the international scenario of women's fair representation and quotas in hiring, and facilities in organisations.

References

1. Acharyya, Rajat (2006). Trade Liberalisation, Poverty, and Income Inequality in India. New Delhi: Asian Development Bank (ADB) INRM Policy Brief No. 10: 1-12 Antonopoulos, Rania (2009) The Current Economic and Financial Crisis: A Gender Perspective. W, p.:UNDP / The Levy Economics Institute of Bard College, Working Paper No. 562.
2. Central Statistical Organisation (CSO) (2007). Annual Survey of Industries. Summary Results for Factory Sector 2005-2006. New Delhi (http://www.mospi.nic.in)
3. Centre for Development and Population Activities (CEDPA) (2001). Adolescent Girls in India Choose a Better Future: An Impact Assessment. W.p., September.
4. Gothoskar, S. 1992. "Struggles of women workers in the pharmaceutical industry in Bombay", in Gothoskar (ed.): Struggles of women at work (New Delhi, Vikas Publishing).
5. Giri, D.V.; Murty, B.S. 1993. "Coal", in C.S. Venkataratnam and A. Verma (eds.): Industrial relations: Current perspectives (New Delhi, Allied Publishers).
6. Government of India. 1969. Report of the National Commission on Labour.
7. ——. 1975. Report of the Committee on Status of Women in India.
8. ——. 1991. Report of the National Commission on Rural Labour.
9. ——. 2002. Report of the National Commission on Labour.
10. ——. 2008. Ministry of Labour and Employment. Annual Report, 2008-09.
11. Gopalan, S. (2002). Towards Equality-The Unfinished Agenda: Status of Women in India, 2001, National Commission for Women, Government of India, New Delhi.
12. Hicks, J.R. (1932). The Theory of Wages, Macmillan, London.
13. www.worldbank.org
14. www.mospi.gov.in
15. http://labour.nic.in/annrep/annrep0809/Chapter-11.pdf
16. NSS (1999-2000), Employment and Unemployment Survey, 55th Round, National Sample Survey Organisation, New Delhi.

17. www.unglobalcompact.org/docs/issues_doc/human_rights/WEPs_CEO_Statement_of_ Support_Signatories.pdf
18. http://data.gov.in/dataset/all-india-and-state-wise-annual-survey-industries-factory-sector
19. www.ethicaltrade.org
20. www.ilo.org/dyn/gender/docs/RES/536/ F932374742/web per cent20gender per cent20manual.pdf
21. Gender Diversity Benchmark for Asia 2011).

8

Economic Crisis and Corporate Social Responsibility

Inderjeet Kaur

Introduction

The financial crisis has brought about dramatic consequences for the world economy and society and we are still witnessing a fragile recovery. A great number of economic and financial experts agree in considering the current world-wide economic and financial crisis to be the worst since the Second World War. The crisis began in the United States with the burst of the subprime mortgage housing bubble, after governmental, supervisory and regulatory authorities undervalued the real risk of the situation. But as the world has become closer, economic and financial markets have diminished in number but increased in size and interconnection. The effects of a financial problem are wide-sweeping and all the world economies suffer the consequences.

The causes of this turmoil are multifaceted. Although many issues remain unclear, there are a couple of conclusions to take from the crisis. The first is that this was a crisis of responsibility, or lack thereof. The second is that it will only be repaired by the re-establishment of trust between companies (especially those in the financial sector) and their stakeholders. Logically, this presents a perfect entry-point for CSR to be finally recognised by the business community as a force for necessary good and long-term sustainability. The emphasis placed by CSR on the role of corporations in the larger social and environmental contract is key in preserving an ideal equilibrium of confidence and responsibility. It is impossible to consider enterprises apart from the society in which they exist. The concept of corporate social responsibility, prescribing that organisations engage in responsible behaviour towards each of their shareholders in the society, has become a necessity today for all businesses although not at the same level for all. Despite the important benefits corporate social responsibility practices have for businesses such as gaining competitive advantage by increasing brand awareness and thus increasing profitability in the long-term, they also require additional financial resources.

Cause of the Crisis

As is now well known, the immediate background to the crisis was the emergence of problems in the US market for sub-prime housing loans in the first half of 2007. Sub-prime loans, in US terminology, are loans that do not meet standard criteria for good credit quality, such as a sound credit history on the part of the borrower, good income documentation and/or a conservative loan-to-valuation ratio. Sub-prime lending became very significant in the United States from around the middle part of this decade; by 2006, these loans were around one-fifth of new housing lending and an estimated 15 per cent of the stock of housing loans outstanding in the United States. The financial sector has been broadly held at least partly responsible for the financial crisis, albeit in the context of regulatory failure and borrower shortsightedness.

Failures in finance were at the heart of the crash. But bankers were not the only people to blame. Central bankers and other regulators bear responsibility, too, for mishandling the crisis, for failing to keep economic imbalances in check and for failing to exercise proper oversight of financial institutions.

The regulators' most dramatic error was to let many big corporates go bankrupt. This multiplied the panic in markets. Suddenly, nobody trusted anybody, so nobody would lend. Non-financial companies, unable to rely on being able to borrow to pay suppliers or workers, froze spending in order to hoard cash, causing a seizure in the real economy. These events sparked a severe loss of confidence, not just in the financial sector, but also across households and businesses.

The meltdown of financial markets in 2008-2009 was the result of institutionalised fraud and financial manipulation. The "bank bailouts" were implemented on the instructions of Wall Street, leading to the largest transfer of money wealth in recorded history, while simultaneously creating an insurmountable public debt.

With the worldwide deterioration of living standards and plummeting consumer spending, the entire structure of the international commodity trade was potentially in jeopardy. The payments system of money transactions was in disarray. Following the collapse of employment, the payment of wages was disrupted, which in turn triggered a downfall in expenditures on necessary consumer goods and services. This dramatic plunge in purchasing power backfired on the productive system, resulting in a string of layoffs, plant closures and bankruptcies. Exacerbated by the freeze on credit, the decline in consumer demand contributed to the demobilisation of human and material resources.

During the current global financial crisis, failures have surfaced in macroeconomic policies and the regulation and supervision of banks and non-banking institutions. It is now clear that agencies involved in regulation, supervision, and crisis management did not always have clear mandates and tools commensurate with these mandates, and that there was a lack of international consistency and coherence of policies.

Corporate Social Responsibility (CSR)

It is impossible to consider enterprises apart from the society in which they exist. The concept of corporate social responsibility, prescribing that organisations engage in responsible behaviour towards each of their shareholders in the society, has become a necessity today for all businesses although not at the same level for all. The call for responsible behaviour heard in the wake of the crisis is long overdue. Indeed, the current crisis is evidence that existing value systems – above all our financial and economic systems – need to be re-examined. Responsibility means, first and foremost, acting now to meet the challenges of the future. We know that the major crises of the future – a battle over natural resources and a global increase in social inequality – will require nations and private industry to act. Accordingly, it is crucial that we reorganise our economic system in keeping with our ecological and social responsibilities, and this will require rethinking how business, the political sphere and society at large interact with one another. As a new mechanism for integrating companies more fully into society, CSR provides a way for private industry to join together with policy-makers and civil society to work for the common good all over the world. Keeping in mind global megatrends in general and the current international economic crisis in particular, the following pages show how CSR, as a management tool, can be helpful in identifying ways to overcome this crisis and meet the social and ecological challenges of the future.The last financial crisis that the world still experiences marked a possible revolution in approaching CSR both from theoretical and practical points of view.

Because of the range and variety of social responsible actions, and the differences in managerial approaches to Corporate Social Responsibility, there is not one generally accepted definition of the term (Barth and Wolff, 2009), but one of the most popularly coined, is the one given by the U.N. European Commission in 2001:

"CSR is a concept whereby companies integrate social and environmental concerns in their business operations and in their interaction with their stakeholders on a voluntary basis. Being socially responsible means not only fulfilling legal expectations, but also going beyond compliance . . ."

CSR is a contested and cluster concept which in essence refers to the expectations that business is:

(i) Responsible for its impacts on society and the environment,

(ii) Accountable for these impacts,

(iii) Conducted in a responsible fashion, and

(iv) Managed within the corporation-society interface.

Dimensions of Corporate Social Responsibility

All ventures use the society's resources with the aim of creating added value and therefore they bear a responsibility against the society. However, we cannot suggest that the extent of this responsibility is at the same level for all businesses. The Pyramid of CSR proposed by Carroll, analysing the dimensions of CSR starting from the basis and extending towards the social responsibility dimension at the highest level, is a generally accepted model in this area. According to this model, the dimensions of social responsibility are:

- Economic responsibility,
- Legal responsibility,
- Ethical responsibility, and
- Voluntary responsibility

Economic Responsibility

The first category that Carroll described is the stage of responsibility that has economic expectations in essence. According to Carroll's model, providing return on investment to business owners and shareholders, creating new jobs and making fair payments to employees, discovering new resources, and promoting creation of new products and services, innovation, and technological progress can be given as examples of economic responsibilities.

Legal Responsibility

The second CSR dimension is the legal responsibilities. Society gives permission to businesses to undertake the role of manufacturer as a part of the "social contract", but also stipulates compliance with the law and various regulations in the course of their operations. In other words, businesses are required to act within the legal framework while they fulfil their mission. In addition to laws restricting the activities of enterprises, certain laws that encourage or enforce CSR activities are also desired by the society.

Ethical Responsibility

Ethical responsibilities include activities and practices that are expected or prohibited to be pursued by the members of the society even if they are not written in the law. For an organisation, ethical responsibilities represent a range of norms, standards, and expectations that reflect concerns such as justice, equity, or protection of incorporeal rights of stakeholders within the context of consumers, employees, shareholders, and society. According to Carroll, economic and legal dimensions of responsibility are mandatory for businesses whereas the society expects the businesses to comply with the ethical dimension. Complying with these rules may vary according to the society the business operates in and those businesses that do not comply with the rules will not be appreciated or be ostracised.

Voluntary Responsibility

Voluntary or charitable responsibilities are the dimension of responsibility that helps recognition of the business as a well-intentioned and philanthropic citizen in the society. The activities in this responsibility dimension that are not legally or ethically mandatory are organised so as to be consistent with the needs of the society in which the business operates. The organisation's allocating its financial resources to activities such as art, education, or culture is included in the voluntary responsibility (Carroll, 1991: 42). Voluntary responsibilities are located in the top level of the pyramid of social responsibility. In comparison to the responsibilities in the lower stages, fulfilment of these responsibilities is not regarded as a necessity by society. The number of enterprises that fulfil these responsibilities is limited and usually they are large-scale enterprises.

Impact of Crisis on CSR

Periods of crisis bring along certain dangers and opportunities, their effects on corporate social responsibility may be in different directions. In this paper, the effects of the crisis on corporate social responsibility activities have been evaluated in the light of the developments following the 2008 global financial crisis. As a result of the identifications regarding the theoretical background for perception of the crisis as a threat or opportunity for corporate social responsibility activities, both two situations are presented together.

The impact of the crisis on CSR pyramid is summarised in two propositions:

Proposition 1: The crisis poses a threat to the responsibility dimensions located at the base of the CSR pyramid.

It is possible to state that the size of the threat posed by the crisis on the responsibility dimensions located at the bottom of the CSR pyramid (Economic and Legal Responsibility) is in parallel with the enterprise's rate of being affected by the crises. In this respect, we need to add that this is more valid for businesses that take measures for being significantly affected or anticipating that they will be significantly affected from the crisis.

Proposition 2: The crisis poses an opportunity for the responsibility dimensions located at the top of the CSR pyramid.

The economic collapse that occurred after the 2008 financial crisis has also led to certain social problems. For example, as mentioned earlier, people losing their jobs caused sorrow in society. This situation has led to a decrease in the reputation of businesses that laid off workers in the crisis period. Due to reasons similar to this, various social phenomena increase their sensitivities in times of crisis. Businesses that desire to make use of the opportunities in the crisis want to put the CSR at the forefront in the crisis periods since it makes positive contributions to the society and the corporate reputation of the businesses. According to Fernández and Souto (2009), CSR that appears to be a threat in times of crisis actually becomes an opportunity. What needs to be done in times of crisis and the needs of CSR practices are quite similar. Using CSR as a business opportunity assists in relocating the business to a better position in the crisis period and overcoming the turbulent environment brought by the crisis in terms of CSR's transforming the fundamental values of the business into an advantageous position by means of the innovation in its essence, having positive effects on endogenous variables such as motivation of entrepreneurial culture, strengthening business strategies, expanding the company's market share, and assuring investor confidence.

Corporate Governance

Corporate governance involves a set of relationships between a company's management, its board, its shareholders and other stakeholders. Corporate governance also provides the structure through which the objectives of the company are set, and the means of attaining those objectives and monitoring performance are determined. Good corporate governance should provide proper incentives for the board and management to pursue objectives that are in the interests of the company and its shareholders and should facilitate effective monitoring. The presence of an effective corporate governance system, within an individual company and across an economy as a whole, helps to provide a degree of confidence that is necessary for the proper functioning of a market economy. As a result, the cost of capital is lower and firms are encouraged to use resources more efficiently, thereby underpinning growth. Factors such as business ethics and corporate awareness of the environmental and societal interests of the communities in which a company operates can also have an impact on its reputation and its long-term success.

OECD Principles of Corporate Governance

The Organisation for Economic Co-operation and Development (OECD) is an international economic organisation of 34 countries founded in 1961 to stimulate economic progress and world trade. It is a forum of countries committed to democracy and the market economy, providing a platform to compare policy experiences, seek answers to common problems, identify good practices and co-ordinate domestic and international policies of its members.

The OECD Principles of Corporate Governance have become an international benchmark for policy-makers, investors, corporations and other stakeholders worldwide.

The Principles also provide the basis for an extensive programme of cooperation between OECD and non-OECD countries and underpin the corporate governance component of World Bank/IMF Reports on the Observance of Standards and Codes (ROSC).

The Principles are intended to assist OECD and non-OECD governments in their efforts to evaluate and improve the legal, institutional and regulatory framework for corporate governance in their countries, and to provide guidance and suggestions for stock exchanges, investors, corporations, and other parties that have a role in the process of developing good corporate governance.

OECD Principles of Corporate Governance were published in 1999 and revised in 2004. The OECD guidelines are often referenced by countries developing local codes or guidelines. Building on the work of the OECD, other international organisations, private sector associations and more than 20 national corporate governance codes formed the United Nations Intergovernmental Working Group of Experts on International Standards of Accounting and Reporting (ISAR) to produce their Guidance on Good Practices in Corporate Governance Disclosure.

The Principles are non-binding and intended to assist member and non-member governments in their efforts to evaluate and improve the legal, institutional and regulatory framework for corporate governance in their countries and to provide guidance and suggestions for stock exchanges, investors, corporations, and other parties that have a role in the process of developing good corporate governance. As such, the Principles are intended to provide a set of guidelines for the implementation of an effective corporate governance framework; not only for companies themselves but rather for an entire system of legislation, regulation and guidelines. The basic areas addressed are:

The Principles presented in the first part of the document cover the following areas:

(I) Ensuring the basis for an effective corporate governance framework;

(II) The rights of shareholders and key ownership functions;

(III) The equitable treatment of shareholders;

(IV) The role of stakeholders;

(V) Disclosure and transparency; and

(VI) The responsibilities of the board.

I. Ensuring the Basis for an Effective Corporate Governance Framework: The corporate governance framework should promote transparent and efficient markets, be consistent with the rule of law and clearly articulate the division of responsibilities among different supervisory, regulatory and enforcement authorities.

II. The Rights of Shareholders and Key Ownership Functions : The corporate governance framework should protect and facilitate the exercise of shareholders' rights.

III. The Equitable Treatment of Shareholders: The corporate governance framework should ensure the equitable treatment of all shareholders, including minority and foreign shareholders. All shareholders should have the opportunity to obtain effective redress for violation of their rights.

IV. The Role of Stakeholders in Corporate Governance: The corporate governance framework should recognise the rights of stakeholders established by law or through mutual agreements and encourage active co-operation between corporations and stakeholders in creating wealth, jobs, and the sustainability of financially sound enterprises.

V. Disclosure and Transparency: The corporate governance framework should ensure that timely and accurate disclosure is made on all material matters regarding the corporation, including the financial situation, performance, ownership, and governance of the company.

VI. The Responsibilities of the Board: The corporate governance framework should ensure the strategic guidance of the company, the effective monitoring of management by the board, and the board's accountability to the company and the shareholders.

Mechanisms and Controls

Corporate governance mechanisms and controls are designed to reduce the inefficiencies that arise from moral hazard and adverse selection. There are both internal monitoring systems and external monitoring systems. Internal monitoring can be done, for example, by one (or a few) large shareholder(s) in the case of privately held companies or a firm belonging to a business group. Furthermore, the various board mechanisms provide for internal monitoring. External monitoring of managers' behaviour occurs when an independent third party (e.g. the external auditor) attests the accuracy of information provided by management to investors. Stock analysts and debt holders may also conduct such external monitoring. An ideal monitoring and control system should regulate both motivation and ability, while providing incentive alignment toward corporate goals and objectives. Care should be taken that incentives are not so strong that some individuals are tempted to cross lines of ethical behaviour, for example by manipulating revenue and profit figures to drive the share price of the company up.

Internal Corporate Governance Controls

Internal corporate governance controls monitor activities and then take corrective action to accomplish organisational goals. Examples include:

Monitoring by the Board of Directors

The board of directors, with its legal authority to hire, fire and compensate top management, safeguards invested capital. Regular board meetings allow potential problems to be identified, discussed and avoided. Whilst non-executive directors are thought to be more independent, they may not always result in more effective corporate governance and may not increase performance. Different board structures are optimal for different firms. Moreover, the ability of the board to monitor the firm's executives is a function of its access to information. Executive directors possess superior knowledge of the decision-making process and therefore evaluate top management on the basis of the quality of its decisions that lead to financial performance outcomes, ex-ante. It could be argued, therefore, that executive directors look beyond the financial criteria

Internal Control Procedures and Internal Auditors

Internal control procedures are policies implemented by an entity's board of directors, audit committee, management, and other personnel to provide reasonable assurance of the entity achieving its objectives related to reliable financial reporting, operating efficiency, and compliance with laws and regulations. Internal auditors are personnel within an organisation who test the design and implementation of the entity's internal control procedures and the reliability of its financial reporting.

Balance of Power

The simplest balance of power is very common; require that the President be a different person from the Treasurer. This application of separation of power is further developed in companies where separate divisions check and balance each other's actions. One group may propose company-wide administrative changes, another group review and can veto the changes, and a third group check that the interests of people (customers, shareholders, employees) outside the three groups are being met.

Remuneration

Performance-based remuneration is designed to relate some proportion of salary to individual performance. It may be in the form of cash or non-cash payments such as shares and share options, superannuation or other benefits. Such incentive schemes, however, are reactive in the sense that they provide no mechanism for preventing mistakes or opportunistic behaviour, and can elicit myopic behaviour.

Monitoring by large shareholders and/or monitoring by banks and other large creditors: Given their large investment in the firm, these stakeholders have the incentives, combined with the right degree of control and power, to monitor the management.

In publicly traded US corporations, boards of directors are largely chosen by the President/CEO and the President/CEO often takes the Chair of the Board position for his/herself (which makes it much more difficult for the institutional owners to "fire" him/her). The practice of the CEO also being the Chair of the Board is known as "duality". While this practice is common in the US, it is relatively rare elsewhere. In the UK, successive codes of best practice have recommended against duality.

External Corporate Governance Controls

External corporate governance controls encompass the controls external stakeholders exercise over the organisation. Examples include:

- Competition
- Demand for and assessment of performance information (especially financial statements)
- Government regulations
- Managerial labour market
- Media pressure
- Takeovers.

Conclusion

This paper intended to identify the link between CSR and the present financial crisis, in order to determine the most important characteristics of the companies' behaviour in this specific context. The present inquiry exemplifies how CSR is subordinate to objectives of economic efficiency, in contrast to statements of companies which need to show adherence to responsible involvement in society. During the crisis, especially, CSR is viewed through the lens of its ability to promote company image and too little in terms of the link between business objectives and needs of society.

The CSR behaviour during crisis varies across industries, companies and countries, but the pattern seems to be quite similar. In general, larger companies are expected not to give up on responsible commitments; industries considered major polluters or being on the scrutiny of different organisations are asked to be more responsible. The pattern that appears to be the most used is a strong discourse in favour of CSR and a strategy that combines short-term measures focused on cost cutting, preserving most visible actions of CSR and a better communication of any responsible action (or which looks as a responsible one) that companies perform during this period. The crisis has to be seen as an opportunity for reinventing, reinforcing, and re-launching CSR. Acknowledging this relationship is a reason itself for sustaining that CSR is an integrative aspect of businesses' and people's lives, and that business is part of the society that requires more than profits. In fact, a responsible behaviour is neither against shareholders' interests nor society's benefits.

Certainly CSR may not be a panacea for all societies' problems or even those caused by economic crisis, but we can consider that many of societies' needs increase during crisis, and corporations are providers of products and services that satisfy those needs in different ways. We are not arguing that it is the duty of corporations to solve this situation, but to consider economic crisis as an opportunity period in which the need for ethical behaviour and Corporate Social Responsibility is greater.

References

http://en.wikipedia.org/wiki/financial _crisis_of_2007

http://theguardian.com/business/2011

http://www.globalresearch.ca/2008

hyttp://en.wikipedia.org/wiki/corporate_social_responsibility
http://www.investopedia.com
http://onlinelibrary.com
http://www.research_methodology.net/carrolls_csr_pyramid
http://ijbbsnet.com/journals/vol_3_feb2012
http://ccsenet.org/journal
http://oecd.org/statistics
http://worldbank.org/rosc.html
http://imf.org

9

CSR and the Indian Corporate Sector

Manmeet Kaur and Punpreet Kaur

Introduction

Corporate Social Responsibility (CSR) has become the buzzword these days in the corporate community all over the globe. Corporations have virtually become the legal owners of the key property in a modern developed society and there are widely held public owned corporations. These corporations are of the people, by the people and for the people and as such owe the people to a considerable extent. This public character underlies the present debate for whose benefit business should be run. There has been a dramatic shift to the predominance of the share-holders interest. Development of new ways of governance coined as corporate governance has been set in motion, and the more extensive and expanded goals of corporate are emerging as CSR.

In any country, with the development of stake-holders model and the emergence of corporate governance, it is being increasingly recognised that a business should be run for a balance of interests of all its stake holders – customers, employees, suppliers, share holders, creditors, government, community, society and so on.

This would amount to a major shift from shareholders value creation to stakeholders' value creation in running of business primarily to create and maintain social harmony, which means those corporations are to be run in the interest of future economic growth and prosperity. For long-term survival and growth in the business the support of society is must and can only be achieved through the practice and maintenance of a high degree of CSR. This will be new definition of performance. In the words of Henry Ford, "The purpose of corporation is to do as much good as we can, everywhere for everybody concerned .... and incidentally to make money", this is the essence of CSR. To stay in business, corporation have to acquire the confidence of the public. You are getting the resources to invest in business from the society, you are earning all your revenues from the society, so why don't you pay back something to society and the community which have contributed to your success. This is CSR.

CSR is no longer mere philanthropy or charity but a hard reality to be put into practice, to invest in and add vitality to business. It is the law which made even the harshest critics of CSR, who always emphasised that "business of business is business" (Friedman, M. 1962) to accept social responsibility. Ethics in business gained momentum after globalisation.

Theoretical Framework of CSR

In very simple terms, CSR is the responsibility of the corporates to the various stakeholders to which a corporate is related in some form or the other; either for capital (owners and shareholders) or for debit or loan (creditors, bankers, financial institutions, public etc.) or for consumption of its products or services (customers); or for production marketing and after sale services of products (employees): or for paying taxes and duties (government and statutory bodies; or for environment ecology and humanity (society at large). All these stakeholders have some expectations from the corporate. It is the commitment of the corporate to satisfy the stakeholders' expectations for their money value or other sacrifices and suffering they might have made towards the benefit of the corporations.

According to Canadian center of philanthropy CSR is a "a set of management practices that ensure the company minimises the negative impact of its operations on the society while maximising its positive impacts."

In the words of Brown, "CSR refers to the obligations of business to pursue those policies, to make those decisions or to follow those lines of action, which are desirable in terms of the objectives and values of our society.

European Union (EU) a major key role player, in furthering CSR in the corporate world has defined CSR as a concept that describes the accountability of a business entity to all relevant stakeholders to: Behave fairly, equitably and rationally in all its actions and proceedings; contribute to the welfare and well being of its employees and their family members, the local community and society at large; Contribute to the economic development of the country while improving standard of living and promoting social development programmes directly or through sponsorship. Do all that is good for the business good for development and good for society. Firm managerial point of view it is a comprehensive set of plans, policies and programmes put into practice by the management in operating the business and its decision-making process that support and facilitate the pursuance of such commitment.

The traditional paradigm of CSR

Till the 1990s, CSR was understood purely in terms of philanthropy or charity. Welfare programmes or initiatives were introduced not as a duty or a responsibility, but as a form of charity that was supposed to indicate the virtues of the company or the organisation.

The practices of business giving continued through the ages, though as economic political and social conditions changed so did business response to social needs. This can be summed up as a shift from merchant charity to corporate citizenship. Four phases in the shift are distinct.

1850-1914:

The first phase was from a more or less purely ameliorative charity for religious reasons and causes during the pre-industrial era (pre-1850) towards the more western form of philanthropy in the period 1850-1914. It was the beginning of industrialisation in Indian and business families began to set up trusts, schools. colleges, hospitals, orphanages and widows homes, art galleries for the welfare of society and the preservation of Indian culture. The early pioneers of industry Jamsetji Jejeebhoy, Jamsedji Tata Premchand Raychand spearheaded the new trend.

1914-1960

In the second phase (1914-1960) which was the golden period of both Indian capitalism and business philanthropy, there was maturing of philanthropic practice. Apart from making political donations for the freedom struggle, business also contributed to many of the social and cultural causes associated with the movement such as revival of Indian art and cultures nationalist education and so on. Many of India's leading businessman GD Birlas, Jamnalal Bajaj, Lala Shri Ram, Ambalal Sarabhai and others come under the spell of Mahatma Gandhi and his theory of trusteeship of wealth.

1960-1980

The next shift came in 1960s which ushered in an era of economic and political troubles and saw the business community operating under several constraints. The state also took an many of the obligation that were traditionally the responsibility of the society as a whole, such as education, care of sick, relief in the wake of natural calamities etc. It led to a corresponding decrease in interest of private philanthropy The high tax regime aided by a deterioration in business morality led to a large expansion in the establishment of charitable trusts for purposes of tax planning. The 1970s thus saw a renewed corporate interest in social concerns and a new element emerged on the philanthropic scene corporate philanthropy as distinct from family business philanthropy.

Post 1980

The post-1980 period saw an upswing in business fortunes due to economic reforms and others factors and with it, a reemergence of self-confidence. It increases both business willingness and ability to give, as well as public and government expectations of business. This contemporary phase, characteristics by corporate citizenship has seen a further swing away from charity and traditional philanthropy towards more direct engagement in mainstreams development concerns and helping society.

Components of Corporate Social Responsibility

More contribution to community building does not make a company socially responsible. A company should take a balance view of the components of CSR and implement the strategies in line with the vision, mission and values of the company.

While companies in North America and Europe are pressured by stakeholders to adopt CSR practices, the Indian companies for have not faced any such pressures. Also Indian companies are still not legally bound to formally report CSR activities like companies in the developed countries. The various components of CSR as per global reporting initiative are:

- Compliance with legal requirements
- Ethical values
- Respect for people and communities
- Environmental concerns

According to a study "corporate philanthropy as business strategy: An Indian perspective" by Laxman Mohanty and Neharika Vohra, publisher in IIMB review:

- Only 12.4 per cent of Indian companies pursue strategic philanthropy as compared to 48 per cent of MNC.
- Charity is pursued by 35 per cent of Indian companies against 62 per cent of MNC.
- Both Indian and multinational corporations give money primarily to support education services, environment, health services, and uplifting living conditions. Support for art and culture, employee volunteering event sponsorship and matching grants (8.0 per cent) are some of the important activities of MNCs but no Indian companies.

How to Implement CSR Strategy

With the fall of Enron and increased awareness of CSR worldwide the corporate all over the world are trying hard to safeguard their reputation with public at large. Today, ethical business practices have assured more importance in order to implement CSR strategy, the following procedure is to be followed:

Understand the relevance of CSR

↓

Build business case for CSR response

↓

Engage with stakeholders

↓

Identify and prioritise key risks

↓

Develop CSR strategies

↓

Develop support policies and procedures

↓

Organisational change (alignment to CSR agenda)

↓

Monitoring performance

↓

Communication

*(**Source:** ICFAI center for management research)*

Emerging Trends in CSR Initiatives

There has been a growing recognition of the fact that corporate should behave like good corporate citizens and as social organisation: they should behave ethically contribute to the economic development improve the quality of life of the community and society at large. Pay taxes and duties regularly and honestly conserve resources, protect the environment and adopt social policies that are progressive and more egalitarian.

In the new millennium there is an increased interest in CSR among corporate and management institutes in India the TATA group is planning to prepare a human development index report which will be the first of its kind in collaboration with the Human Development Resource Centre (HRDC) of the UNDP and is trying to create new standards for accountability along with lines of the Human Development Index (HDI). This will make it simpler for the group companies to report in their balance sheets about the work being done an other from its besides business.

The management schools are counted to trains a breed of new age managers who will e socially responsible. Even as corporate are embanking upon defining good corporate citizenship in terms of management practices the management schools are developing modules and full fledged programmes to build up a deep sense of corporate responsibility for e.g. the Management Centre for Human Values (MCHV) in Indian Institute of Management (IIM) Kolkata, deals extensively with issues related to business ethics and CSR. Other institutions such as IIMB, offers students project-oriented election and compulsory modules on corporate governance and CSR.

ONGC

ONGC has been contributing generously towards CSR initiatives all along as a responsible corporate citizens and is willing to add more dimensions to this noble area in future also. Along with its regular activities on this front, it has adopted some villages for providing urban amenities in rural areas in tune with our honourable president's idea of PURA (Provision of urban amenities in rural areas) and sufficient resources have been allocated for various activities.

PURA involves creation of four types of connectivity

- **Physical:** Road, transport and power;
- **Electronic:** telecom facility, internet, information technology and communication services
- **Knowledge:** education and training in schools and colleges, technical and scientific education and job-oriented training and development;

- **Economic:** Agriculture, horticulture, dairy farming and animal husbandry involving improvement of methods of farming, breeding of plants animals etc.

ONGC PURA initiative plans to setup PURA in states where it carries out its operation substantially, and such states include Assam, Nagaland, Andhra Pradesh, Maharashtra and Gujarat. A trust has been constituted by ONGC called ONGC PURA trust with a corpus amount 10 crore. The trust is to function in partnership with NGOs energy research institutes, rural agriculture banks, private sector and professionals.

In April 2005, ONGC launched its first PURA project in Tripura in a village named Maichara in East Kalabaria – 150 km away from the state of Agartala. Urban facilities provided include power house, community centre, school library (knowledge and electronic connectivity) and community kitchen (Physical connectivity).

In Addition to PURA scheme CSR initiatives in general cover intimation promotion, sponsorship, management and provision of amenities and facilities towards various activities relating to:

- Education centres including schools, colleges, scientific and technical institutes;
- Provision of relief to different charitable hospitals clinics, crèches etc.

NTPC

NTPC possess a long tradition in the history of CSR initiatives in all the important areas of community development, power generation, upliftment of the neglected segment of the society disaster management etc.

Community Development

Contributing to community development through several programmes and schemes in its core operating zones has always been a unique features of NTPC. It has contributed towards development of infrastructure, provided education and medical facilities to the people of the neighbouring areas of its operating zones on a regular basis. As a part of infrastructural development it has developed local roads, pavements helped in building marketing centres, community building and sponsored several such other community development programmes around its power stations.

In the field of education, sports and cultural development some of the facilities extended by NTPC include:

- Adoption of primary school.
- Special drive for women education, girls education and adult education by running special centres for these purposes.
- Encouragement of rural culture through organising several cultural programmes.
- Arranging different healthcare programmes like eye camps, general medical camps, surgical camps.

Power Generation

There are many remote villages in India where infrastructural facilities for providing electricity is very negligible. In a drive to provide power in such areas NTPC is committee to set up small generators of about 10 kW capacity at or near the end users to meet their power requirements. As a part of CSR initiative NTPC has successfully experimented the setting up of small power generators based on biomass collected from the villages and is willing to extend such technology to more villages in the days to come.

Upliftment of Neglected Society

NTPC has constituted as trust to work for the development of the physically disabled and poor people so that their standard of living may be raised. NTPC arranges for loan for assisting various income generation endeavours of such physical challenged people so that they can maintain their livelihood.

Natural Calamities

As a part of CSR policy NTPC has committed itself to stand by the side of the national government with all sorts of assistance during natural calamities like Tsunami, earthquakes, floods, etc. to mitigate the sufferings of the affected people and to generously provide help in various rehabilitation programmes connecting thereto.

TATA Group

The company's philanthropic activities can be dated back to as early as 1982 when Jamshedji Tata established JN Tata endowment scheme to provide higher education for deserving Indians. Since then 3500 Tata scholarships have been awarded; recipients include KR Narayana (former President of India) and Dr Raja Ramanna (Renowned scientist). JRD Tata believed that social responsibility of his companies should be institutionalised. Thus, in the 1970s, the group amended its articles of association according to which the group shall be mindful of its social and moral responsibilities to the consumers, employees, shareholders society and the local community for all its major companies.

That TATA steel rural development society (TSRDS) was established for rural development in 1979. Today it covers 700 villages in and around TATA steel's diverse business operations in Jharkhand and Orissa. TSRDS helps communities for the improvement of their QOL by implementing a number of relevant programmes and hands over the management to the trained members of the community in education, healthcare and sanitation services, family planning, drinking water, irrigation, agriculture animals husbandry, adult literacy, vocational training. It also encourages rural industry, entrepreneurship and handicrafts.

TATA steel presented the first corporate sustainability report in July 2002 which served as benchmark and a confidence builder for other TATA companies. It also has formed group resource under the TATA council for community initiatives (TCCI) on corporate sustainability and a strategy to assist other TATA companies on CSR.

TATA have spent Rs 1.5 bn on social services (highest by any corporate house in the country) the thirst areas has been rural development which included community health, basic education and vocational training. It also spends on basic infrastructure and disburses money through various charitable struts and relief and reconstruction societies.

Infosys Technology

Infosys formed in 1981 by NR Narayana Murthy, follows a socially responsible and sustainable path in conducting business. Even during the boom time of the 1990s when the stock price of IT companies were skyrocketing the company believed in sharing the wealth with the society and its employees. This practice of the company stems from the personal belief of Murthy to give back to the society more than what it gave him. It also substantiates the role and motivation of the CEO and the top management in making the company a responsible corporate citizen.

Murthy believes that corporations should ensure transparent disclosures in to investors to attract global capital; show fairness in dealing with employees to retain them; ensure customer satisfaction to win confidence and loyalty; ensure fair dealings with their supply chains; and should be ethical to government by paying all the taxes. Infosys has won many awards such as Best employers to work for in India, Golden Peacock award for excellence in corporate governance in the Global category by the world council for corporate governance, London and corporate citizenship award by the economic times.

The Infosys foundation was formed to focus on healthcare, primary education, social rehabilitation and rural uplift, art and culture, Sudha Murthy, (Narayana Murthy's wife) chairperson of the foundation, its taking a leadership role in influencing corporate India to discharge their social responsibilities besides focusing on profit generation. The foundation began its activities in Karnataka in 1996. The activities have extended to Tamil Nadu, Andhra Pradesh, Maharashtra, Odisha and Punjab. According to a recent report Infosys spends about Rs 50 mn on social activities.

AV Birla Group

For the last 50 years the AV Birla Group has been contributing to the poor in and around its plants across India. Previously, the group used to give money in charity. However, the late Aditya Birla felt that giving money to the poor was not a long-term solution. He felt that social projects should be self-sustainable in the long run. The group's welfare-driven initiatives are channelled through the Aditya Birla Centre for community initiative and rural development spearheaded by Rajashree Birla (Aditya Birla's wife). All the group companies are dedicated to social development. Hindalco, a group company has won the federation of Indian chambers of commerce and industry (FICCI) SEDF social responsiveness award 2001.

The group is engaged in innovative projects involving the development of rural youth and employment generation, education and training and healthcare projects helping the disabled people, social cause like widow remarriages, dowry less marriage and women empowerment programmes. The group also undertakes sponsorship of arts and Indian culture, which are needs based. The Birla Academy of Art and Culture, setup in Kolkata in 1962 treasures art works and exquisite exhibits and has evolved into one of India's premier institutions of art and culture.

Others

Though still largely voluntary several companies in the public sector as well as in the private sector have come forward with their CSR initiatives on different focus areas to implement various activities and programmes for the welfare and well being of the people, community and society. The areas generally covered are healthcare, family planning, education, sports, employment generation and other areas of socio-economic development. Some large companies in the public sector like ONGC, Coal India, SAIl BHEL, etc. are used to spending up to five per cent of their pre-tax profits towards social upliftment and community development. Midday meals for school children are being sponsored by corporates like Infosys, ARB India etc. Apart from our government efforts to provide balanced nutrition to younger generation the Ambanis' in Gujarat have adopted a number of villages for community development and rehabilitation programmes.

In future there will be a manifold increase in such imitative and more and more companies will join has to shoulder a wide range of social responsibilities to supplement the government effort in this direction and a new Indian will be borne. The task is difficult but together we can!

Conclusion

John D Rockefeller says, "Think of given not as a duty but as a privilege". It seems Indian companies have accepted that business is not just making money. This is evident from their involvement in various community development activities. In the Indian context the philanthropic outlook of CSR appears to have vanished and the companies are seeing it as an opportunity to serve the society thereby contributing their share for the well-being of their society in which they exist.

CSR is a dynamic concept and it will keep on changing as per the new requirements of society, to push it to achieve higher standards. The new paradigms of CSR are emerging. The concept of CSR has been perceived by the business organisations in many ways. Some consider it as a strategy; some have taken it as an opportunity for innovation. To succeed in business a company must maintain global standards of CSR conduct towards all stakeholders and should recognise the fact that CSR is key driver of sustainable growth and long-term value creation.

Now message is very clear, performance of the companies would no longer be measured by the financial bottom line only but by the triple bottom line; economic, environmental and social and a balance should be maintained among these and are to be operated within accepted norms of propriety equity fair play and a sense of generosity and thereby build stakeholders confidence. Let us wish and hope that CSR becomes a part and parcel of business activity more by design than by default.

References

"Ethics and CSR: Do they Accelerate or Hinder Business Growth?" *Accounting world,* September 2007, p. 48.

Cooperative Social Responsibility audit: Strategy or Compulsion? The Emerging Trend of Indian Cooperatives, Vrajlal K. Sapovadia.

Corporate Social Responsibility- the new Performance Measure of Corporates, *The Accounting World,* November 2006, p. 45.

George A. Steneir and John F. Stenier, "Business, Government and Society", Mcgraw-Hill, 1997.

K. Aswathappa,"Essentials of Business Environment" p. 510.

Peter Prattey, "The Essence of Business Ethics", Prentice Hall of India.

Social Asset Accounting: Is the Creation of Social Asset, a part of Corporate social Responsibility Initiatives, *The Accounting World,* January 2008, p. 53.

South Asian Journal of Management, Vol. 14, No. 1, pp. 105-119, 2007.

The ICFAIAN Journal of Management Research, Vol. 6, No. 9, pp. 48-53, September 2007.

www.ssrn.com

10

Understanding the Ethical Context of Organisations: Strategies to Improve

Dr Simranjit Kaur and Monika Sharma

Introduction

Ethics is a philosophical term derived from the Greek word 'ethos' meaning character or custom, this definition is germane to effective leadership in organisations in that it connotes an organisation code conveying moral integrity and consistent values in service to the public (Ronald R, Sims, 1992). Ethical behaviour is that which is morally accepted as 'good' and 'right' as opposed to 'bad' or 'wrong' in a particular setting (Ronald R. Sims,1992). Employees' behaviours are not only influenced by their values, but also the culture and mechanism of the companies. (Jackall, R 1988) declaims that unethical actions of managers do not result from individual moral deficiencies alone, but are encouraged by the bureaucratic structure of modern corporations. Even the most upright people are apt to become dishonest...when placed in a typical corporate environment

(Frederick). Thus, companies play an important role to encourage managers to behave ethically, and management control systems can shape the ethical behaviour. Academic scholars are writing a lot of books on business ethics and asking business managers to practice themselves and to implement those ethical principles in their organisations. Universities in almost all countries in the world are teaching 'business ethics' as a compulsory or elective course to their students. They believe that today's students are future managers and executives of different business organisations. So, they should know the importance of business ethical principles starting from their student life.

Ethics is the study of morality. It is the value that is worth pursuing in life. It is honourable behaviour. Ethics is relative. What is honourable in one society may not be honourable in another. It depends on several factors: world views, descriptive values and moral values. It is a function of the environment. What one salesperson may consider being an unethical marketing behaviour, another salesperson may perceive it as an aggressive marketing strategy.

Ethics can be illustrated with the popular story of a millionaire who built an Olympic size swimming pool for his evening enjoyment. He filled the pool with many crocodiles of different types and sizes. His own idea of enjoyment is to watch these crocodiles swim every evening. At the completion of the construction of the swimming pool, he invited all the elites of the city to its dedication. As people were eating and drinking, an announcement was made by the host, over the public address system, that if any young man was bold enough to swim across the swimming pool, he would be given one of two things: a real estate that worths $1 million or his only beautiful daughter in marriage. Before he finished his announcement, a young man jumped into the swimming pool, to the surprise of everyone, swam across the pool and got out without a single bruise on his body. The millionaire ran to him, gave him a big hug and asked him what he would like to receive out of the two. The young man said he did not want any of them and that the only thing he wanted was, he wanted to know the bastard who pushed him into the swimming pool. That is ethics. The young man told the truth. He did not want any of the two rewards promised by the millionaire because he did not, on his own, jump into the pool. He was pushed by an unknown person. The millionaire too behaved honourably. He did not believe anyone could jump into the swimming pool to swim across. Since somebody did, he was still willing to stand by his words. He did not say he was not willing to give his only daughter in marriage to a stranger.

Unethical Behaviours

The media feeds us with information of unethical behaviours in our environment revealing the unethical social issues that demand our attention. The newspaper accounts of unethical behaviours in business have raised concerns about business ethics which have led to studies on their causes in organisations (Carroll, 1978, 4). These unethical behaviours are from unsavory individuals that have no moral character. In 1961, the survey conducted by Reverend Raymond C. Baumhard S. J., showed that there was a very high concern about ethical behaviours. That concern is higher today (Brenner and Molander, 1977, 57).

The incidence of employee misconduct and behavioural deviancy in organisational settings and their potentially adverse effects have attracted considerable attention. Diverse terms have been used to refer to such behaviour namely, unethical behaviour (Jones, 1990), deviant behaviour (Robinson and Bennett, 1995), dysfunctional behaviour (Griffin *et al.*, 1998), counterproductive behaviour (e.g., Fox and Spector, 1999), anti-social behaviour (e.g., Robinson *et al.*, 1998), or organisational misbehaviour (e.g.,Vardi and Wiener, 1996). These forms of (mis)behaviour cover a wide range of actions from withholding effort to disobeying orders or drug abuse in the workplace. They have been classified as interpersonal and organisational according to whether they are directed towards individuals or the organisation, and also according to degree of gravity ranging from minor (showing favouritism) to serious (stealing, verbal abuse) (Robinson and Bennett, 1995; Bennett and Robinson, 2000). They have been further divided into extra-organisational and intra-organisational behaviours (Jones, 1990) depending on where they occur, and production deviance, property deviance and personal aggression depending on the target (Robinson and Bennett, 2000). Some authors point to a difference between destructive deviant behaviour and unethical behaviour. The former has been defined as a set of intentional acts conducted by employees that violate organisational norms and potentially harm the organisation or its members (Bennett and Robinson 2000; Robinson and Bennett, 1995). The latter, by contrast, is 'either illegal or morally unacceptable to the larger community' (Jones, 1991: 367). However, Vardi and Wiener's (1996:151) definition of organisational misbehaviour covers both organisational norms and social values and 'standards of proper conduct'. According to Appelbaum *et al.* (2006), while unethical behaviours centre upon the breaking of societal rules, deviant behaviours centre upon the violation of organisational norms. Nonetheless, this distinction is not always clear. Behaviours motivated by loyalty to the organisation, such as engaging in deceitful advertising practices or dumping toxic waste in a river, may be considered unethical but not deviant. Conversely, disobeying such orders or blowing the whistle on them may be deemed ethical but deviant, depending on the point of view (social or organisational). The Civil Service Commission of Philippines defined an unethical behaviour as any behaviour prohibited by law. In a dynamic business environment, a "large gray area" exists that makes it difficult and unclear to distinguish what is ethical. An unethical behaviour would therefore be defined as one that is not morally honourable or one that is prohibited by the law.

Unethical behaviour is any action that is aimed at taking advantage of another without their knowledge or consent. Most define this as manipulating someone without their permission. Unethical actions are not necessarily illegal. Many behaviours will fall in the classification including corruption, mail and wire fraud, discrimination and harassment, insider trading, conflicts of interest, improper use of company assets, bribery and kickbacks, compliance procedures, ethical relations with others, disciplinary action, fraud, illegal business donations, patent infringement and product liability (Barrcus and Near, 1991, 12). Unethical behaviours that stimulated interest in ethics include Watergate events, Lockheed Scandal, the 1972 United States presidential election, illegal business donations and bribery of foreign officials in order to induce business abroad (Carroll, 1978, 5). Today, the most common ones are false communication, collusion, conflicts of interest, gifts and kickbacks, health services providers' unfair practices, insider trading, discrimination and harassment, and embezzlement.

False Communications

False communications fall into various categories. They include falsification of auditor's or controller's report or any form of manipulation that does not tell the whole truth. These include cheating on tax returns or inappropriate depreciation schedule and wrong expenses (Brennan Jr., Valtz, Shallenberger and Stanton, 1961, 164). Feeding the public with wrong report of the organisation's business performance to make the organisation look good is another common practice, seen in some of the high profile cases in the United States.

Collusion

Collusion, especially with competitors, to fix prices, is an unfair business practice today. This could be considered stealing from customers. However, there are differences of opinion on whether or not price fixing is stealing from customers (Brennan Jr., Valtz, Shallenberger and Stanton, 1961, 174).

Gifts and Kickbacks

Some organisations do not allow their employees to receive gifts from clients during normal course of business. Those who do, generally provide guidelines on limitations as to the amount an employee can receive as gift. Sometimes a buyer may request for kickbacks or entertainment which, if not provided, may lead to the loss of the customer. An employee frequently receives pressure from the management to behave unethically or to obtain profitable business at any cost, which may include the use of any possible dirty tricks. The employees who desire to be retained or promoted have no choice but to dance to the tune of the management. This is because there were cases of those who refused to behave unethically the way management instructed and were fired or nearly fired (Brennan Jr., Valtz, Shallenberger and Stanton, 1961, 165).

Conflict of Interest

Conflict of interest occurs when ones private interest interferes or appears to interfere in any way with the interest of the organisation. According to Sliglitz, it can be argued that there is no conflict of interest because, based on Adam Smith's view, the individuals, when pursuing their own self-interest are actually pursuing the general interest of society (Sliglitz, 2003, 2). Some examples of conflicts of interest are:

- diverting from the organisation for personal benefit, a business opportunity,
- using the organisation's assets for personal benefit,
- accepting any valuable thing from the organisation's customers or suppliers, and
- having a financial interest in an organisation's competitor.

Unethical Practices in the Healthcare Sector

There are three common unethical practices in the Health Care Sector. The first is refusing to provide healthcare services to the patients who have no medical insurance. Some health centres do not admit patients who have no insurance unless they can provide evidence that they have the ability to pay for the health service. The second unethical practice in the healthcare sector is over treating patients to boost income. The third is doing surgery at surgical centres instead of the hospital so that the doctors do not have to "pull call at any hospital" (Weber, 2003, 6).

Insider Trading

Insider trading is an unethical behaviour which occurs when a person who has access to confidential information uses or shares the information for securities trading purposes or any other purpose except the conduct of regular company business. The confidential information of the company are not to be used for achieving personal gain neither are they to be disseminated directly or indirectly, to friends, family members and other outsiders who may in turn trade on or misuse the information.

Discrimination and Harassment

Discrimination involves not providing equal opportunity in employment on merit but on other basis such as race, sex, national origin, age, religion, or any other basis not related to the job. Harassment is a derogatory comment or unwelcome sexual advances (FS Networks, Inc., 2004, 3).

Wrong Doing

A large number of people, including top management, are involved in wrong doing both in the public and in the private sectors.

Why People Behave Unethically

Dedicated employees, who are usually honest, sometimes behave unethically because of four rationalisations: that no one will ever find out, that the behaviour is not really illegal, that it is in the best interest of the organisation, and that the organisation will protect them. Although the costs of unethical behaviour are hard to measure, they can add, according to research, more than 20 per cent to the cost of doing business. The costs will include low wages, unemployment, and poverty. If top management wants to improve organisational performance, they must stand firm that ethical methods are the only ways business should be done.

Causes of Unethical Behaviours

The study that was commissioned by American Management Association (AMA) and which was conducted by the Human Resource Institute (HRI) using 1121 managers and Human Resource experts as participants, revealed that the leading cause of unethical corporate behaviour is "pressure to meet unrealistic business objectives and deadlines." The study also showed that the second leading factor that causes unethical behaviour is the desire to further one's career while the third leading factor is the desire to protect one's livelihood (Schwartz, 2006, 1) and (Mac Do, 2006, 1).

Job pressure, according to the study, causes employees to engage in unethical behaviours that include cutting corners on quality control, covering up incidents and lying to customers. Ignorance is another major cause of unethical behaviours. The study of (AMA) and (HRI), (MacDo, 2006, 1), revealed that the ignorance that the acts are unethical and not knowing the seriousness of the consequences when caught, are causes of unethical behaviours. Competition for scarce resources, power or position can cause individuals to engage in unethical behaviours. Hosmer emphasised that an attempt to improve their corporate competitive positions made managers to take immoral actions (Hosmer, 1987, 439). Bazerman and Banaji felt that the cause of the unethical behaviours in organisations is the presence of a "few bad apples" among organisational actors (Bazerman and Banaji, 2004, 111). The primary cause of unethical behaviours can be traced to lack of maintaining the type of consistent leadership that is necessary for running an ethical organisation. This exposes the employees to opportunities that make them engage in unethical behaviours.

Recommendations

The National Defense University proposed three ethical responses to unethical behaviours in their "Strategic Leadership and Decision Making:" exit, voice and loyalty. With respect to "exit" it is recommended that if one can not live with the behaviour, or the behaviour does not meet one's ethical standards, one should leave. The second response, "voice," is to express discomfort with and opposition to the unethical behaviour. The third response, "loyalty," supports the idea of remaining in the organisation and trying to change it instead of leaving (National Defence University, 1986, 8).

In order to restore and maintain a culture that upholds honest and ethical behaviours, the organisational leaders must verbally promote ethical environment and relentlessly "walk the talk," by making ethical behaviour part of the organisation's agenda. They need to establish codes of business conduct to guide employees' behaviours. There should be the establishment of annual business ethics training for the employees and a good whistle blowing mechanism. Since job pressure was identified as major cause of unethical behaviour, in order to reduce the pressure, communications and commitment by top management are recommended (McShulskis, 1997, 24).

Conclusion

Today, there is a tremendous loss of confidence in corporate conduct and there is an urgent need to work towards restoring it. Although ethics education seem to produce limited evidence of changing behaviours, the commitment of management to monitor annual ethics education for all employees will produce the desired favorable results. There should be clear communication to the employees of what are honourable and expected behaviours in the organisation. They must maintain and stand firm on a clear cut policy that ethical methods are the only way of doing business.

References

Baucus, Melissa S. and Near, T. Janet P. 1991. "Can Illegal Corporate Behavior Be Predicted? An Event History Analysis." *Academy of Management Journal*. 34 (1), 9-36.

Bazerman, Max H. and Banaj, Mahzarin R. (June, 2004). "The Social Psychology of Ordinary Ethical Failures." *Social Justice Research*, (17) 2. 205, 111-115.

Betz, Joseph (1998). "Business Ethics and Politics." *Business Ethics Quarterly*. 8 (4), 693-702.

Brennan, John J. Jr.; Valtz, James J.; Shallenberger, John. B.; and Stanton, Vincent P. "How Ethical Are Businessmen?" (July – August, 1961). *Harvard Business Review*. 6-19, 156-176.

Brenner, Steven H. and Molander, Earl A. (January – February, 1977). "Is the ethics of business changing?" *Harvard Business Review*. 57-71.

Carroll, Arehin B., (Summer, 1978). "Linking Business Ethics to Behavior in Organisations" *SAM Advanced Management Journal*. 4-11.

Civil Service Commission of Philippines; (May, 2000), "Enhancing Ethical Behavior in Business and Government," http://www.csc.gov.ph/

Collins, Denis. (April 24, 2007). "Assessing, Sustaining, and Enhancing an Ethical work Culture." Midwestern Intergovernmental Audit Forum.

F.S. Networks, Inc. (2004). Code of Business Conduct and Ethics. http://business.edgewood.edu/dcolllins. www.f5.com/pdf/f5code-of-ethics-204.pdf.

Gellerman, Saul W. (July – August, 1986). "Why good managers make bad ethical choices." *Harvard Business Review*. 85-90.

Hosmer, LaRue J. (1987), "The Institutionalisation of Unethical Behavior." *The Journal of Business Ethics*, 439-447.

McShulskis, Elaine (July, 1997). "Job stress can prompt unethical behaviour," *HR Magazine*. 22-24.

National Defense University. (1986). "Strategic Leadership and Decision Making." //www.au.af.mil/au/awc/awcgate/ndu/strat-ldr-dm/comt.html. 1-10.

Stiglitz, J.E. (2003) "Ethics, market and Government Failure, and Globalisation." www.2.gsb.Columbsa.edu.

Trevine, Linda Klebe and Youngblood, Stuart, A, (1990). "Bad Apples in Bad Barrels: A Canal of Ethical Decision-Making Behavior." *Journal of Applied Psychology*. 75 (4) 378-385.

Velasquez, Manuel (1996). "Why Ethics Matters: A defense of Ethics in Business Organisations." *Business Ethics Quarterly*. 6 (2) 201-222.

Wasden, Lawrence. (July, 2007). Office of the Attorney General, Idaho. Ethics in Government Manual.

Weber, David O. (2005). "Unethical Business Practices in U.S. Health Care Alarm Physician Leaders." Special Report: Ethical Debates/Ethical Breaches. www.google.com/search? 1-11.

11

The Relevance and Role of Professional Ethics in Teaching

Taruna Narang and Nidhi Palta

Introduction

Education is a tool for total human development and if any one aspect of human personality is ignored, it can result very adversely. Without imparting values and morals in education, human development will be incomplete. Values and morals are inbuilt in human being and education should help in the improvement of human character and recognition of inner purity, so the education system should emphasise the values and morals along with the other development. If we look at the ancient education system of India we can realise that our education system was very prosperous, value based and skills oriented.

In ancient time, the teachers were concerned about the total improvement of students, which included their intellectual level, understanding abilities, awareness of responsibilities, regard for elders, appreciation for cultural heritage and responsibility towards their fellow classmates. However, these above qualities are not seen in the present education system due to various changes such as modernisation, industrialisation, urbanisation, privatisation, globalisation as well the influence of Western culture accompanied by many other problems and evils in Indian society that cause declining ethical values in Indian education system .This system has definitely increased the literacy rate but not helped in creating educated persons in society and as a result, it does not produce ideal citizens in the country. The main objective of Indian students has remained how to take their degree, earn money and be careerist without consideration of ethical values and national spirit in their life. This is the reason why the profession of a teacher has become so challenging and demanding.

A teacher is a person who provides education to students. The role of the teacher is often formal and ongoing, carried out at the school or other place of formal education. The teaching profession comprises of teacher's obligations, devotions and competencies towards teaching. If the teacher acquires the required competencies and commitment, they can perform their multiple tasks efficiently; it will inculcate a high level of learning in students from all aspects.

Education is considered to be the soul of society passing from one generation to next and teaching as a profession requires expertise, knowledge and special skills. It also expects a sense of personal commitment to education and the welfare of society. Teachers must view teaching as a profession, possible only if they realise the importance of professional attitude. There are large numbers of good teachers but the problem of ethical issues still prevails.

Ethics

The word ethics has been derived from the Greek word 'ethos' which means character and from Latin word 'Mores' which means customs. It is about correctness or incorrectness of human activities. Ethics play a very significant role in achieving educational aims. Ethics is a set of concepts and principles that guide us in determining what behaviour helps or harms sentient creatures (Paul and Elder, 2006). Ethics is also about practical judgment- the application of principles to issues and decisions.

Ethics encompasses theoretical and practical reasoning. Theoretically, ethics is the analysis of the language of ethics, forms of ethical reasoning and the objectivity of moral principles. Practically, ethics is "applied ethics" the study of principles for such domains as corporate governance, scientific research and professional practice (Dimock and Tucker, 2004).

Webster's *New World Dictionary* defines ethics as "conforming to the standards of conducts of given profession or group". If you are going to live in a particular society then it becomes very important that what that society considers to be ethical and what to be unethical. Ethical considerations arise every day in our life. If we understand the meaning of ethics we expect to lead our lives productively and benefit those with whom we interact.

Professional Ethics

Professional ethics is the application of standards of ethics on important events of professional life. A professional individual assures the public about his ethical sensitivity through his activities and behaviour. These ethics help to maintain the integrity of the profession. Every professional is answerable to his clients, employers, state and society. But in professions other than teaching it is not the duty of professionals to educate or mould the clients. The teaching profession is such a profession in which teacher has to educate and develop the individuals harmoniously in all aspects.

Relevance and Role of Professional Ethics in the Teaching Profession

Ethics in teaching refers to specific values, standards, rules and agreements adopted by the teachers. The teacher is considered to be more teacher as he has a wide range of responsibilities regarding teaching, building up the character of individual, making them productive members of the society and channelling their energy in positive directions and finally helping them to grow and develop into good human beings. The effective teacher must not only be skillful in promoting in learning and should be the preacher of good values, but also the model of ethical behaviour. The picture of teaching has changed with time, with change in values, with cultural and social change and along with the essence of ethical aspect has widened. But the image of the teacher is becoming light and he is being criticised with regard to his duties. There are many unfavourable aspects of professional ethics being followed by teachers like, giving preference to domestic work, indulging students for doing his works, helping in cheating and advocating tuition system.

It has been realised that like all other professions the teaching profession should also have its own Code of Professional Ethics which ensures its dignity and integrity. Right of Children to Free and Compulsory Education Act 2009 entrusts teachers with some responsibilities to be internalised by them in the performance of their duties. The Code of Professional Ethics for Teachers provides a framework of principles to guide them in discharging their obligation and duties towards students, parents, colleagues, and community. Increased awareness of the ethical awareness governing the teaching professional is essential to ensure "professionalism" among teachers. The debate concerning the ethics of education that took place in United States at the beginning of twentieth century has gained global interest in the past two decades. This very debate targets the moral behaviour of the teacher and the morality that children learn in school.

In 2001, Educational International (EI) officially entered this debate when the Declaration on Professional Ethics (DPE) was adopted by EI's 3rd World Congress held in Jomtein, Thailand. The document was further updated at its Fourth world Congress in Porto Alegre, Brazil in 2004. The DPE is mainly intended as a blueprint of EI affiliates own guidelines. It is complementary to the International Labour Organisation (ILO) Declaration on Fundamental Principles and Rights at Work (1998) and draws on the UNESCO Recommendation concerning the Status of Teachers (1966) and the United Nations Universal Declaration of Human Rights (UDHR) (1948).

Its Objectives are :

- To raise consciousness about the norms and ethics of the teaching profession.
- To help increase job satisfaction in education.
- To enhance status and self-esteem.
- To increase respect for the profession in communities.

National policy on education (1986) emphasis the preparation of a Code of Ethics for teachers. It will ensure that the teachers are working and behaving according to the standards and norms. It will enhance their commitment towards profession and also improve their effectiveness. There are many reasons due to which the Code of Ethics has been thought to be prepared such as:

- Enabling teachers to meet the demands of teaching profession.
- Enabling teachers to do justice to the roles and responsibilities.
- Providing teachers with guidelines for linkages with the community.
- Guiding teachers to be always fair and unjust in treatment.

Teaching in true sense, is an attempt to influence the behaviour of pupils. In this regard the most important thing is the personal examples of the teachers. His or her dedication towards the profession influences society. According to Chopra (1998), the teacher has to acquire three characteristics:

- Expert knowledge of the subject.
- Special training in core teaching skills and method.
- Continuous in service growth to do full justice to their work.

A teacher must take above written characteristics seriously and inculcate the best possibility to be the model for their students.

Obligations of Teachers

Obligation is defined as the responsibility of an individual. It is always ethical. A person who has chosen teaching as a profession accepts the obligation to perform activities in the line of duty and in accordance with the standards of the profession. A professionally committed teacher takes pride in improving his noble profession. He strives to follow the code of obligations. Teachers are expected to perform their activities in the following dimensions given by NCERT:

- In relation to students.
- In relation to parents and guardians.
- In relation to professional colleagues and other professional organisation.
- In relation to management and administration.

Obligations in relation to students:

- Treat all the students with love and affection.
- Respect the values of being just and impartial to all students irrespective of their caste, creed, religion, sex, economic status, disability, language and place of birth.

- Respect basic human dignity of the child in all aspects of school life.
- Make planned and systematic efforts to facilitate the child to actualise his/her potential and talent.
- Adapt his /her teaching to the individual needs of the students.
- Refrain from subjecting any fear, trauma, anxiety, physical punishment, sexual abuse, and mental and emotional harassment.
- Maintain the confidentiality of the information concerning students and dispenses such information only to those who are legitimately entitled to it.

Obligations towards Parents, Community and Society

- Establish a relationship of trust with parents/guardians in the interest of the all round development of students.
- Desist from doing anything which is derogatory to respect of the child or his/her parents/guardians.
- Strive to develop respect for the composite culture of India among students.
- Keep the country uppermost in mind, refraining from taking part in such activities as may spread feelings of hatred or enmity among different communities, religious or linguistic groups.

Obligation in Relation to Professional Colleagues and Other Professional Organisation

- Strive for his/her continuous professional development.
- Create a culture that encourages purposeful collaboration and dialogue among colleagues and stakeholders.
- Take pride in the teaching profession and treats other members of the profession with respect and dignity

- Refrain from engaging himself/herself in private tuition or any other private teaching activity.
- Respect the professional standing and opinions of his/her colleagues.

Obligations towards Management and Administration.

- Bind himself with rules and regulations.
- Become a link between students and management.
- Help the management in developing strategies.
- Share policies and organise programmes.
- Be respectful to higher authorities.

Apart from these obligations the teacher has to take care of other obligations which change with respects to time and situations.

The Ethical Responsibility of Teaching Institute or College

Efforts to lift the level of the standards of ethics and morals have always been regarded as necessary and desirable and should always be so regarded. This does not mean that every individual should become a "reformer" or that all of our institutions- educational, governmental and commercial should become ethical societies, seeking reform. An educational institution is not a commercial enterprise; it is not in the business of manufacturing or selling commodities. It is not a political party. It is not a religious place. Its concern is with the life of the mind with the attainment of intellectual excellence. But if we combine intellectual excellence with a peaceful soul than it is called education with moral ethics which produces a complete human being.

Conclusion

A teacher has great duties to perform for the betterment of the society. The teacher must have a sound philosophy and social sensitivity and concern for social and human rights. If the teacher follows ethical values, his conduct and behaviour becomes respectable and socially acceptable. His behaviour in a positive manner will influence students to follow him and be like him. Hence he becomes the ideal for students. His wrong step can make the students to turn into the dark. Different academicians, regulating bodies, develop these obligations, but implementation is on the shoulders of teachers. A teacher through the profession of teaching could take the future of the nation, i.e. its students, towards the right direction and hence, make society to be a better place to live in.

References

Chuan-bao, T (2006). On the change of concepts: From Teacher's Occupational Ethics to Professional Ethics, *Front.Educ. China*. 3, 439-446.

Chopra, R.K. (1998). Code of Professional Ethics for Teachers. New Delhi: NCERT

Prasad, H. and Prasad. (1998). Towards Professionalisation of Education, *University News*, 43(18)

Sahoo, P.K., *et al.* (2010). Professionalism in Teacher Education. New Delhi: Concept Publishing Company Pvt. Ltd.

Yadav, P.S. (2013). Ethical Concern : Leads to Quality of Social Work Research, *University News*. 51(20), 13-16.

NCERT, (1997). Code of Professional Ethics for Teachers. New Delhi.

12

Adopting Sustainable and Eco-friendly Mechanisms of Human Development

Dr Anurag Sankhian

Introduction

The increasing population of India, as well as its all-round development, means that the pressure on available utilisable water resource is also increasing at a fast pace. The dwindling availability of fresh water resources is a major issue before the Government of India. Many parts of the world were also facing the same problem. Keeping in view the deepening crisis throughout the world, the United Nations declared the year 2003 as the International Year of Fresh Water and subsequently the General Assembly at its 58th session in December 2003 agreed to proclaim the years 2005-2015 as the International Decade for Action, "Water for Life". The per capita water availability in the country is reducing progressively due to increase in population and rapid growth and industrialisation. The Indian population, which was 361 million in 1951, increased to 1.03 billion in

2001, and is expected to be 1.27 billion by 2016 as per Census of India. The per capita availability of fresh water was 5177 cubic meters during the year 1951, has dropped to 1816 cubic meters as per 2001 census and further reduced to 1545 cubic meters as per 2011 census (Press Information Bureau, 2013). India has 17.31 per cent (1.27 Billion) of the world's population but the global water resource available within the country is only four per cent of the global water resources. An analysis of the water availability on a per capita basis indicates that India is now under classification of 'water stressed', i.e., less than 1,700 m^3/person/year.

The demand for establishing hydroelectricity projects is one of the priorities of the state and central governments for meeting the power requirement in the country. As socio economic development of any country depends upon the power sector. The power sector makes a direct and significant contribution to the economy in terms of revenue generation, employment opportunities and enhancing the quality of life. The energy consumption levels of any country are directly related to its development status. The high energy consuming countries are high in the ladder of development in comparison to low energy consuming countries. Twenty per cent of the world population living in the industrialised countries consume 60 per cent of the energy and remaining 80 per cent of population has to manage within 40 per cent of total energy (Shahi, 2003). Hydro power is a clean energy resource. But throughout the world the hydroelectric power generation has reduced from 21 per cent in 1973 to less than 17 per cent in 2000 due to various reasons. Presently the country is able to exploit only 25 per cent of the total potential. Himalayan states including Jammu and Kashmir, Uttarakhand and Himachal Pradesh have tremendous hydro power potential. 50,000 MW hydroelectricity generation initiatives were launched by the Central government in the year 2003. 162 hydroelectric schemes were identified with an aggregate installed capacity of 50,560 MW. These hydroelectric schemes are located in sixteen states of the country. 106 schemes aggregating to about 39,000 MW are located in only four states namely, Himachal Pradesh, Uttarakhand, Jammu and Kashmir and Arunachal Pradesh. These projects are being executed under 11th and 12th Five Year Plans from 2007 to 2017. It shows that all these states are going through the process of large scale hydro projects development and challenges associated with the construction of hydro projects. In the phase of hydro power projects development, the construction activities play havoc with the nature, destroy natural water resources, damage drinking water supply schemes, indulge in illicit felling of forest trees etc. The present paper is an attempt to show the condition of the local population in the state of Himachal Pradesh, struggling for water share and stressing for adopting eco-friendly mechanisms during the process of development of the hydro power projects. The study shows the resentment of the local nearby villagers of Palampur town struggling for their water share rights and fighting the loosing battle in stopping the state government and private players developing the hydro projects in the state of Himachal Pradesh.

Himachal Pradesh: Blessed with Vast Hydroelectric Potential

Himachal Pradesh has been blessed with vast hydroelectric potential in its five river basins, namely, Yamuna, Satluj, Beas, Ravi and Chenab. The state is drained by nine river systems. The Satluj is the largest river system in the state with a total catchment area of 20,398 km^2. The Beas is the second most important river with a catchment area of 13,663 km^2. The Chenab River is also known as the Chandrabhaga, it is the largest river in terms of water volume with catchment area of 7850 km^2. The Yamuna flows in the south-eastern part of Himachal Pradesh, the Yamuna is fed by a number of tributaries before flowing into Uttar Pradesh. The Ravi River originates from an amphitheatre type basin in the Dhauladhar Range, turning southwards cutting a deep gorge through the Dhauladur hills. The Ravi stretches 130 km before leaving the state into Punjab and Pakistan.

Through preliminary hydrological, topographical and geological investigations, it has been estimated that about 23,000 MW of hydel potential can be exploited in the state by constructing various major, medium, small and mini/ micro hydel projects on these five river basins. So far projects with aggregate capacity of 7,728 MW have been commissioned and plan is to exploit the entire potential by the end of the 12th Plan. The target for the 10th plan was 2090 MW, 11th plan 9155 MW and 12th Plan 5027 MW (Lohumi, 2011). Out of this only 467 MW, just six per cent of the total potential exploited, has been harnessed in the state sector by H.P.S.E.B. The Basin-wise details of the assessed potential (Project capacity MW) are as; Yamuna 811, Satluj 10355, Beas 5339, Ravi 2952, Chenab 2973, New Identified 570 (Total 23000 MW). In the current financial year 2011-12, Government of Himachal Pradesh expect to add 2090 MW in the system with commissioning of the thousand MW Karcham Wangtoo, Malani-2 (100 MW), Budhil (70 MW), Chamera-3 (231 MW), Parvati (520 MW) and some other small hydel projects. By the end of the Twelfth Plan, Himachal Pradesh is expected to have over 17000 MW of generating capacity. For generating hydel power generation in a phased manner, Himachal Pradesh formulated its own hydro power policy in 2006. This policy seeks to safeguard the interest of the people of the state along with delicate ecology and environment. Policy also stress and ensure development of local area, during the construction stage mandatory provision of 1.5 per cent of the project cost has been kept in state policy.

Sector wise detail of hydro power projects in Himachal Pradesh

The Sixth International Hydro Power Convention was organised on 26-27th April 2011 at Shimla on the theme,

"Speeder Harnessing of Hydropower Potential in Northern Himalaya". The Chief Minister of Himachal Pradesh and State government officials revealed that the State Government is actively working in the direction of developing hydropower projects in the state in a phased manner by involving both Central Government PSUs and private sector developers. The proposed distribution of nearly 23,000 MW, in various sectors is likely to be 17 per cent State sector, 39 per cent Central/Joint Sector, 38 per cent private sector and remaining five per cent is less than five MW. It has been observed that Hydro power projects construction and development is full of complexities and challenges. The only positive side of the development of hydro power projects is that they cause very less air pollution in the long run in comparison to the plants generating electricity by burning fossil fuels. Carbon dioxide is just produced during the initial stage of construction of the project.

Table 1: Sector-wise Detail of Hydropower Projects/Assessed Potential (MW)

Sr. No.	*Particulars*	*State Sector*	*Central/ Joint Sector*	*Private Sector*		*Total*
				Up to 5 MW	*Above 5 MW*	
				(through HIMURJA)		
01	Projects Commissioned	467	5490	105	610	6672
02	Under Execution	1125	2763	413	1685	5986
03	Allotted and Under Execution	2201	841	721	3972	7735
04	To be allotted	101	-	60	1756	1917
05	Abandoned	-	-	-	690	690
	TOTAL	**3894**	**9094**	**1299**	**8713**	**23000**

Source: Himachal Pradesh Economic Survey Report 2010-2011.

The cost of operating a hydroelectric plant is nearly immune to increase in the cost of fossil fuels such as oil, coal, natural gas etc.

Rivers and catchments in Himachal Pradesh are under severe stress. Large development projects, especially hydro-power projects combined with climate changes and receding glaciers are expected to adversely affect the natural eco-system and also run off the characteristics of potential rivers. A study by the Asian Development Bank (ADB) on "climate change adaptations in Himachal Pradesh — sustainable strategies for water resources" has painted a grim picture of the overall water scenario in the state, strongly recommending a master plan for conservation of water resources and sustainable management of the existing sources. The report concludes that climate changes are happening faster than the mitigation and adaption measures taken by the government or agencies.

Neogal River Life Line of Palampur Town

Located in the Kangra Valley of Himachal Pradesh, the Neogal is a perennial tributary of the Beas River. The Beas River and its tributaries are considered to have the potential to generate 4500 MW of power, most of which is now being tapped by way of 23 Large, Small and micro hydel projects, on the river. The geographical coordinates are: Longitude: 760-30′-40" E and Latitude: 320-05′-15" N. It originates from the Dhauladhar hills and is a snow and rain fed river, forming the Neogal Watershed comprising of riverine terraces and plains fields as well.

The key characteristic of the river is the heavy dependence on it for drinking water and irrigation. A traditional, well developed *Kuhl* (irrigation channel) system exists in the Palampur area, whereby villages have channelised water of the Neogal River for irrigation purposes. Almost 40 such large and small *kuhls*, managed as common property resources, have catered to the irrigation needs of over a 100 villages in the watershed (Baker, 2005). Apart from this, Palampur town and villages up to 30 Kms downstream – close to 30000 of a population depend on the water of the Neogal River and Bohal spring (originating in the same watershed) for drinking. Close to twelve water supply schemes are being run by the IPH on the river.

Micro Hydro Power Projects on River Neogal

Neogal Hydro Electric Projects are a run-of the river type hydro power project on Neogal Khad, a tributary of river Beas in Kangra District of Himachal Pradesh in the northern part of India. Two of the projects, coming up on the Neogal River include the 15 MW projects being developed by Om Power Corporation and another 4.5 MW project by the Astha group of companies. The project is a run of the river scheme with a 3.5 km long headrace tunnel. The TEC to the project was first accorded in 1991-92 by the CEA. At the time the project was planned by the Himachal Pradesh State Electricity Board. The MoU was signed with M/s Om Power Corporation in Aug.1993. Implementation Agreement was signed in July, 1998. Draft PPA between the company and the HPSEB has been signed in Dec.1993. The installed capacity of the project is 15 MW and expected gross energy generation is 87670 MW per annum. The project activity would utilise potential energy available in flowing water for power generation. Natural river bed fall and water available at the location are the inputs for power generation. The electricity produced at 11 kV will be stepped up to 33 kV and evacuated through 12 km long 33 kV transmission line to HPSEB sub-station at Dehan. The project activity comprises civil structures such as diversion weir, intake structure, headrace tunnel, surge shaft, penstock, power house, tailrace channel, switchyard, electro-mechanical components such as 2 Nos of Pelton turbines, synchronous generators, transformers, switchgear equipment, power plant control systems and fire fighting equipment. Project cost is estimated at Rs 982.77 millions. The project is expected to generate net energy of 82848 MW to India's NEWNE Power Grid. The Project will avoid 69599 tons of CO_2 greenhouse gases (GHGs) annually by avoiding future capacity expansion of fossil fuel-based generation. These projects will have far reaching impacts on the ecology as well as local livelihood systems of the region.

Carbon Credits Claim Issue under Clean Development Mechanism (CDM-UNFCCC)

The CDM is one of three "flexibility mechanisms" established by the Kyoto Protocol (The other mechanisms are emissions trading and joint implementation).[1] The Clean Development Mechanism (CDM) of the Kyoto Protocol allows industrialised countries with a greenhouse gas reduction commitment to invest in emission reducing projects in developing countries and claim credit for the reductions achieved. Under CDM industrialised and developing countries pay the extra cost of upgrading the technology in developing countries. In turn they get credits for the account of CHG emissions mitigated by the technology upgrade. In theory, this will help reduce compliance costs, while providing new financing for sustainable development in the south. By using the CDM Mechanism developed nations will be able to sell their technology to the developing and underdeveloped nations. By doing so they will be getting double benefit as they will be able to meet the Kyoto requirements by getting the needed credits in their account and second they will be in a position to continue with their own rate of green gases emissions (Aggarwal, 2009). Additionality is the crucial test of whether a CDM project results in emission reductions that are in excess of what would have occurred under a business as usual scenario, and thus whether the project should be awarded carbon credits that can be used by an Annex I party to meet its Kyoto commitments. To keep credit prices down, Annex I [2] buyers are promoting a so-called "environmental" additionality test that, perversely, validates business as usual projects and will create a large loophole in the Annex I [2] emission reduction targets through the generation of spurious credits. There are currently over 4200 CDM projects in the pipeline (not yet all approved) which would represent a total of 2.9 billion tons of carbon dioxide equivalent in reductions by 2012. A total of 1596 CDM projects have been registered (approved) as of April 2009, up from 39 projects a mere four years ago. These projects will represent a total of 1.6 billion CERs (known as Certified Emissions Reductions or CERs) by the end of the Kyoto Protocol's first commitment period (2012).[3]

In the case of Neogal power project, strong objections have been raised by the local population on carbon credits claim applied under CDM. The construction company applied for claiming the carbon credits under the Clean Development Mechanism (CDM), to the United Nations Framework for Climate Change Convention's (UNFCCC) Executive Board highlighting the project activity's contribution to sustainable development of the region. The present CDM claim of the company is in the validation stage. Project participant views that project activities will contribution to sustainable development of the local region. The project will contribute positively as per the indicators stipulated by Ministry of Environment and forests, Government of India in the interim approval guidelines for CDM project; (a) Social well-being (b) Economic well-being (c) Environmental well-being and (d) Technological well-being. There would be minor environmental impacts due to the construction of the project activity. Financial provisions are made for various environmental mitigation measures. This project is in line with the "National Conservation Strategy and Policy Statement on Environment and Development" of the host country.

1 Annex I Parties listed here: http://unfccc.int/essential_background/convention/background/items/1346.php

2 The Mechanisms under the Kyoto Protocol: The Clean Development Mechanism, Joint Implementation and Emissions Trading. Website of the UNFCCC Secretariat, http://unfccc.int/kyoto_protocol/mechanisms/items/1673.php

3 Registry of CDM Methodologies: http://cdm.unfccc.int/methodologies

Environmental Challenges Associated with Neogal Hydro Power Project

Hydroelectric projects are being strongly opposed by the local population and environmentalists over the fallout of impounding of rivers and ruthless tunnelling of hills and large scale deforestation and drying up of water sources. The environmental fall-out apart, over-exploitation of hydropower potential will have long-term implications on the lives and livelihood of the local population, as the main rivers will virtually disappear from the scene (Lohumi, 2011). The ongoing construction of the Neogal hydro power project is creating lot of environmental challenges along with ongoing conflict between the construction companies, local administration and various state government departments related with the problems. Hydro power generation can be a top-most priority of the central and state governments but large scale development of such projects has brought lot of problems and challenges to the local simple living villagers of the Himachal Pradesh. It has also brought a lot of changes in the traditional living systems and life of the local peoples.

The project construction companies' claims that project activity would generate social well being by generating additional employment to an extent of 200 persons during construction period and 20 persons during operation period for both skilled/ unskilled people. Due to various developmental activities in the vicinity of project area quality of life will improve in the area. But the local population feels that construction activity will generate employment opportunities only for some time which will not be permanent in nature. These construction companies also claim that the construction would mobilise investment to an extent of about Rs 982.77 million in this region, which otherwise would not have occurred in the absence of the project activity. Moreover, 1.5 per cent of the project cost would be allocated for Local Area Development by the project proponent to take up improvement measures in education, healthcare facilities, welfare facilities, preservation of culture etc. The 12 per cent free power to government will ensure overall economic improvement in the state. All such claims were also rejected by the simple living peoples of the Palampur valley as the construction work has disturbed the living of the local population in one way or another. In the case of environmental well being the company claims that project will meet the energy requirement of the region in an environmental-friendly manner as presently major portion of energy requirement of the region is met from fossil fuel based power generation. In this case the local population feels that state is already producing lot of hydro power which is enough for the need of the state and reject the claim of dependence of state on fossil fuel based power generation. Concerned Citizens and Environment Action groups of Palampur have submitted detailed objections on the proposal by OM Power Project to claim Carbon Credits under the Clean Development Mechanism (CDM), to the United Nations Framework for Climate Change Convention's (UNFCCC) Executive Board highlighting the serious damages caused by the 15 MW project to the Neogal river valley and the water supply systems on it. Action group states that Neogal River is the only source of the drinking water and irrigation. The whole Palampur belt and nearby villages totally depend on this river for their basic need of water. River also feeds the traditional, well developed *Kuhl* (irrigation channel) system existing in the Palampur area, whereby villages have channelised water of the Neogal River for irrigation purposes. Almost 40 such large and small *kuhls*, managed as common property resources, have catered to the irrigation needs of over a 100 villages in the watershed.

Apart from this, Palampur town and villages up to 30 Kms downstream – close to 30000 populations depend on the water of the Neogal River and Bohal spring (originating in the same watershed) for drinking. Close to twelve water supply schemes are being run by the Irrigation and public health department of the state government on this river. But the construction work of the present project has generated serious impact due to new road construction which resulted in frequent occurrence of landslides and further resulted in negative impact on the several irrigation channels and water supply schemes which have got blocked or damaged due to the debris and loose falling boulders. The Kirpal Chand *kuhl* and the Diwan Chand *kuhl* have been the most affected. The two *kuhls* together meet the irrigation needs of over 100 villages. These have either become heavily silted or have been blocked or dried up. For the last three years the Irrigation and Public Health Department, which officially governs these channels, has billed an amount of Rs 3 crores as penalty to the project proponents, who have paid up only about 9 lakhs as of 2013 which has been utilised for some repair work. The bigger question, however, will be the supply of water to these two major *kuhls*, which draw their water from the location between the two projects being constructed by Om Power Corporation and Astha Construction Company. People also question the availability of the enough water to cater to the Hydropower project requirements as well as those of the drinking and irrigation water supply schemes in near future.

Another environmental challenge generated is due to unscientific cutting of hill rocks by these construction companies which was also reported by hundreds of villagers from three panchyats of Bundla and Kandi areas who are continuously protesting against the construction of hydro power projects near Bundla. The local population is demanding immediate suspension of construction of power project as it had completely disturbed the ecology of the region. In the construction process, hundreds of trees had also been axed along with over two hundred hectares of land had been affected by cutting, whereas the construction company was allowed to restrict its activities only to fifteen hectares. The construction company was allowed to cut only four hundred trees but at project site more than one thousand green trees had been affected by the reckless cutting of hill rocks. The damage to the ecology is clearly visible as eyesores on a verdant landscape from tens of kilometres away. Om Power Corporation, executing a 15 MW hydro power project has been fined Rs 64 lakh due to violation of environment norms and cutting excess number of green trees. It was also charged that the company has excavated hills haphazardly and dumped debris in the local irrigation channels and the Neugal River resulting in a serious water crisis in the entire region. In June 2009, the project was fined an amount of Rs 12,90,000 for the damages caused to the forest areas due to the muck dumping. The views expressed by the forest officials reveal that, "Most hydropower projects are violating environment laws but, the government is adopting a pick-and-choose policy to take action. It reacts only when there is a protest by local communities." (*The Tribune*, 03.11.08).

The hydro power project work is also having negative impact on the economical condition of the locals. The location of the project site is in the lower slopes of the Dhauladhar range of the region. The area is significantly forested with oak, kail, chir, pine and cedar trees. The forests are used by Gaddis for grazing their sheep, though habitation is sparse in the region. The households located close to the power house site with Surdi village being the most impacted as a result of the dust, landslides (due to construction of road), loss of grazing land (due to unapproved dumping of debris) and also due to the loss of some of their land for the road construction. While they were compensated for the land, there has been no compensation/mitigation for the various other impacts these poor families have been facing. Another of the critical impacts was destruction of their water tank as a result of the debris from the road construction. The hydro power project work is also having negative impact on the health conditions of the local population residing in the Palampur municipal area. The waste from the workers colonies of the project at the power house as well as the tunnel site is flowing untreated into the Neogal River and contaminating the water. The heavy siltation and muck in the water, especially during the monsoons makes the river highly turbid and the water dangerous for drinking despite filtration. People residing in the (30 families) in Saan Village (also part of Bundla Panchayat) are being affected by the dust and breathing problems. The Palampur Citizens Environment Welfare Forum as well as residents of the Bundla Panchayat and users of the *kuhls* has raised need to be protect and conserve the Dhauladhar range and the Neogal river to ensure clean and sustained development of the Palampur valley. This all clearly shows that, fast pace of human development, stress on natural resources and neglecting the eco-friendly methods are playing havoc in the beautiful Palampur valley of the Himalayan regions.

Conclusions and Suggestions

Hydro power is clean energy resource and in this case, Himachal Pradesh is rich and blessed with vast hydroelectric potential (23,000 MW) in its five river basins, namely Yamuna, Satluj, Beas, Ravi and Chenab. The hydro power projects with aggregate capacity of 7,728 MW have been commissioned and plan is to exploit the entire potential by the end of the 12th Plan (2022). This shows that large scale construction of these projects will take place in near future. Hydro power projects construction and development is full of complexities and challenges. Neogal Hydro Electric Projects are a run-of the river type projects on Neogal River, a tributary of river Beas in Kangra District of Himachal Pradesh in northern part of India. Installed capacity of the project is 15 MW and expected gross energy generation is 87670 MW per annum. The ongoing construction of the Neogal Hydro power projects are creating lot of environmental challenges along with ongoing conflict between the construction companies, local administration and various state government departments related with the problems. There is a need to protect and conserve Neogal River to ensure clean and sustainable development of the Palampur valley. The major problems associated with the construction of the power project in the valley include, environmental degradation, large scale deforestation, adverse health impacts on residents near project site, blockage of Irrigation Channels, Impact on Drinking water quality and Supply, and Muck dumping in forest areas.

The local population is demanding immediate suspension of construction of power project as it had completely disturbed the ecology of the region. All such developments bring total change in the life of the local population and neglect on the part of government along with environmental challenges is a big reason of resentment in the rural simple living population of the hill state. The paper also suggests adopting sustainable and eco-friendly mechanism of human development for saving the natural beauty of the Himalayan valleys.

References

Aggarwal, Anil (2009). Climate Change- A Challenge to India's Economy, Centre for Science and Environment, New Delhi, http://www.cseindia.org

Baker, J.M. (2005). The Kuhls of Kangra: Community-Managed Irrigation in the Western Himalaya, Permanent Black, Delhi, India, p. 271.

Clean Development Mechanism Backgrounder (2009). Status Report and The Kyoto Protocol (see Article 12), Climate Change PEW Centre, http://unfccc.int/essential_background/kyoto_protocol/items/1678.php

Climate change- What is all about? (2009). European Communities, http://www.nfcc.in

Gregg, Marland *et al.* (1999). National Carbon dioxide Emission from fossil fuel Burning, Cement Manufacture and Gas flaring, Oak Ridge Laboratory, USA.

Lohumi, Rakesh (2011). Be Judicious, The Tribune, September 23, Chandigarh, India.

Press Information Bureau (2013). Per capita water availability, Ministry of water resources, Government of India, release vide ID 82676, 26 April, 2012.

Sharma, Ashwani (2011). HP Water resource under severe stress finds ADB study, Development projects, mega hydro-power projects, climate change adaption's, Posted on May 11 2011, Shimla, http://adb.org/documents/books/cca-himachal-pradesh.

The Road to Copenhagen: India's position on climate change issues (2009). Public Diplomacy Division, Ministry of External Affairs, Government of India, http://www.meaindia.nic.in

The Tribune (2008). Power Company told to Suspend Construction, Monday, November 3, Himachal Edition, Chandigarh, India

13

Environmental Protection Vis-a-Vis Sustainable Development-A Global Challenge

Amit Kashyap and Shashi Bala Kashyap

Introduction

This paper discusses the United Nations World Charter for Nature 1982, and partly the UN Declaration on environment made in 1972. In this context we need to study the state of our national environment and take stock of what changes have occurred during past more than fifty years of freedom, the state, nation and the people.[1] In the light of changes, we shall study how the importance of integration of law and science itself has given new dimension to the growth of our civilisation. Modern international law also acquired a multidimensional role in world society. The purpose of law and science is to achieve a peaceful and dynamic world order. Both disciplines have important roles for the protection of natural environment. Therefore, we have to study the provisions of the United Nations World

Charter For Nature[2], 1982, a Charter which has important message for the state, nation and the people of India. Without a wholesome human environment, we cannot provide people an opportunity for social and spiritual growth.

Man Out of Harmony With Nature

While we assess the United Nations World Charter for Nature, it is realised that man's activities have created a situation where man is out of harmony with nature. Technology has driven man to a new life-style globally. Long ago, Rabindranath Tagore, said that in ancient times man lived in harmony with nature. Modern man has set aside the law of nature, as Tagore says:

> We expected that the laws of nature should be held in abeyance for our convenience. But now we know better. We know that law cannot be set aside, and in this knowledge we have become strong. For this law is not something apart from us; it is our own.[3]

This principle of unity is the mystery of all mysteries. The existence of a duality at once raises a question in our minds, and we seek it solution in the one. When at last we find a relation between these two, and thereby see them as one in essence, we feel that we have come to the truth.[4]

With reference to environment problems in India, we have pointed out that "population, human settlement, transportation, energy, resources and developments are some important parameters that have bearing directly and indirectly on the environment policy of India."[5]

The Unity of Law and Science and a Biologist View of the World

The purpose of the law in the larger view is to seek a social order based on harmony of people. In science, the aim of various disciplines is to comprehend harmony in nature. For example, ecology is defined as the relationship of living organism and their adaptation to environments. It is a definition which is close to law as law seeks to determine relationship between people. I have written a detailed article on the ecological approach to international law. This approach seeks an eco-management of global life.[6] In physics, Einstein says:

> The supreme task of the physics is to arrive at those universal elementary laws from which the cosmos can be built up by pure deduction. There is no logical path to these laws; only intuition, resting on sympathetic understanding of experience, can reach them.[7]

In law also, jurists say that life of law is based on experience. As Justice Holmes said in 1986:[8] "...your business as thinkers is to make plainer the way from some thing to the whole of things, to show the rational connection between your fact and the frame of the universe."[9]

Thus, law and science are two aspects of human experience, one based on the social order and the other on the natural systems. It is but obvious that in a scientific world society, law and science should interact. In the recent period a synthesis of law and science seems to be taking place towards the evolution of a biologist view of the world. Later in this paper I will see how the biologist imprint is found in two major legal instruments drafted by mankind through the United Nations for the protection of global environments and for a new world order.[10]

The UNESCO held a world symposium on science and synthesis on the tenthdeath anniversary of Einstein and a great biologist, Chardin. The most important outcome of the symposium was that the world is based on relatedness of the natural laws. Therefore, the interdependence of the biological and ecological laws seems very important for environment management.[11]

Another Nobel Laureate scientist, Ilya Prigogine, has in the recent period laid emphasis on the "intellectual construction" needed in comprehending laws of nature and the concept of reality."[12] Prigogine refers to the dialogue between Einstein and Rabindranath Tagore on the meaning of reality. He agrees with the view expressed by Tagore. As he says: "Curiously enough, the present evolution of science is running in the direction stated by the great Indian poet." Tagore had said during his discussion with Einstein[13] that truth was based on the comprehension of the observer (we may call experience); whereas Einstein believed that science had to be independent of the existence of any observer.[14] The conversation between Einstein and Tagore was regarding the nature of Reality.[15]

In the context of the environment movement of our times, an intellectual construction of law and science is needed to provide a biologist view of the world which would be close to the reality of nature, and which would provide harmony in the universe.[16]

The Global Environment Movement and the UN Declaration on Human Environment, 1972

In response to the call of history, the United Nations representing the concern of whole of mankind made a "Declaration of the United Nations Conference on the Human Environment, 1972."[17] The United Nations Declaration was an epoch-making step taken by mankind to safeguard environment and ensure good life on earth. The major emphasis of the Declaration was to seek harmony of man with nature and to promote knowledge about the laws of nature. The Declaration in particular introduced a new biological revolution in the world. It said that Man is both creature and moulder of his environment, which gives him physical sustenance and affords him the opportunity for intellectual, moral, social and spiritual growth, said the Declaration "is a major issue which affects the well-being of peoples and economic development throughout the world...". The Declaration warned about "evidence of man-made harm in many regions of the earth: dangerous levels of pollution in water, air, earth and living beings; major and undesirable disturbances to the ecological balance of the biosphere....".

The UN Declaration while referring to the problems of developing countries said that their environmental problems are caused by underdevelopment. And, it warned that "the natural growth of population continuously[18] presents problems on the preservation of the environment, but with the adoption of appropriate policies and measures these problems can be solved. Of all things in the world people are the most precious. It is people that people social progress, create social wealth, and develop science and technology, and, through their hard work, continuously transform the human environment."[19]

The Declaration called for a cooperative approach of man with nature. It said that "A point has been reached in history when we must shape our actions throughout the world with a more prudent care for their environmental consequences". It highlighted the role of modern man vis-à-vis the environment as follows:

"There are broad vistas for the enhancement of environmental quality and the creation of a good life. What is needed is an enthusiastic but calm state of mind and intense but orderly work. For the purpose of attaining freedom in the world of nature, man must use knowledge to build in collaboration with nature a better environment."

The Declaration of the UN has called for rational planning which is essential to avoid conflict between the needs of development and the need to protect and improve the environment. It called for planning of human settlements with a view to avoiding adverse effects on the environment. It called to pursue vigorously demographic policies which are without prejudice to human rights and which the governments deem appropriate. Above all, the Declaration has asked the peoples of the world to enlarge education on the environment, undertake scientific research and cooperate on bilateral and multilateral basis to avoid damage to the environment.

The UN World Charter for Nature 1982

The world Charter for Nature drafted by the United Nations in 1982 makes a clear scientific admission for the first time in modern period that man is a part of nature.[20] Man is dependent upon the natural systems for his life and growth. Man is also a part of single species. Leading anthropologists like Rene, Dubas, and Margaret Mead have laid worldwide emphasis on the fact that all men are part of the species with instinct for cooperation and love. Mead provides a global view that diversity of life of man in nature only strengthens the unity of mankind; because mankind is one single species, as she says:

"There has been a continuing interest in dealing with wholes; with mankind as a species, the single hominid-species now existing on this planet, with many variations in climate and breeding conditions, but still essentially one species, exhibiting complete intra-species fertility and hybridisation between varieties as a source of strengthen."[21]

It is profitable to recall for the Charter for Nature that the world is one large ecological unit with unity in diversity of life in the nature. As I have submitted earlier:

"Biologically and ecologically the world is one interdependent unit. In this single unit, all the living organisms have an inter-relationship and adapt to the local environment. Laws of nature operate in this unit to keep nature's ecological balance. We may refer to nature's carbon cycle, the oxygen cycle, the radiation balance of earth, and similar scientific phenomena which are related to the global ecological system."[22]

Therefore, the UN Charter for Nature is to be analysed in the light of the world being one large ecological unit, comprising of single species of mankind along with other living organism, living in an interdependent world, with unity in the diversity of nature. Even the UN Declaration on Human Environment of 1972 contains biological and ecological principles which shape life on this planet. Biologist view of world seems the major focus in contemporary civilisation.

Another scholar Victor Ferkiss writing on ecological humanism says that it is the global philosophy these days.[23] Ecological humanism "is based on the conviction that man, if he is to continue to exist and if he is to fulfill himself as a human being, must live in a conscious ecological relationship with nature and with other men, and the ecological perspective on the natural order provides a necessary analogue for the social order."[24] Professor Ferkiss makes some very useful following observation on man and universe: "Universe is a process moving forward in time. Life and all its attributes consist of processes. Life is an emergent property of life. Both have evolved in the course of development of universe. Processes which maintain themselves over time are structures, that is patterns of order which persist because of relative equilibria—among their constituent elements. Change in nature is the result of the interrelated changes among the elements of natural systems. The world and humanity are one entity, one system, in equilibrium. Earth is humanity's only home; humanity is one people in relationship to the earth".[25] Ferkiss has cited works of eminent authors on the ecological perspective and political theory, the biological foundations of political science, etc.[26]

The World Charter for Nature[27]

The UN World Charter for Nature of 1982 is therefore an important document for mankind. It represents the global philosophy for life and living on this planet. It says "mankind is part of nature and life depends on the uninterrupted functioning of natural systems which ensure the supply of energy and nutrients". That "civilisation is rooted in nature, which has shaped human culture and influenced all artistic and scientific achievement", and "living in harmony with nature gives man the best opportunities for the development of his creativity and for rest and recreation". The Charter outlines that, "Energy form of life is unique-warranting respect regardless of its worth to man", that "man can alter nature and exhaust natural resources by his action or its consequences". The charter says that, "lasting benefits from nature depend upon the maintenance of essential world peace.[28]

The Environment Protection Act of India, 1986

Taking note of the United Nations Declaration of 1972 and the UN Charter for Nature 1982, the Government of India has enacted The Environment Protection Act, 1986.[29] The Preamble to this act states that "whereas decision were taken at the United Nations Conference on Human Environment at Stockholm in June, 1972, in which India participated, to take appropriate steps for the protection and improvement of human environment"; and whereas it is considered necessary further to implement the decisions aforesaid in so far as they relate to the protection and improvement of environment and the prevention of hazards to human beings, other living creatures, plants and property...", the Environment Protection Act, 1986 is enacted.

The Act of 1986 gives effect to the decisions of the UN Conference of 1972, provides for environment protection and improvement, prevents hazards to human beings and all life including the plants, thus combining law and biological sciences in a unique fashion, and, generally, sketching a biological view of the world. The biologist view is based on the interrelatedness of ecosystems. It considers all mankind belonging to single species *homo sapiens*. The biologist interpretation of nature easily fits with the diversity of nature including human beings, falling within a unified natural order. It is not proposed here to refer to each constituent part of Indian Environment Protection Act of 1986. Suffice to mention that it has set a pattern-to-shape national life in conformity with the laws of nature as Tagore had envisaged, and keeping due regard to the synthesis of law and science in all policy-making for environment management.[30]

Some Conclusions

The attempt in this paper is to combine law and science for environment protection and management which provides a new global perspective, a new paradigm. It may provide a new structure for a scientific revolution with emphasis on the biologist view of the world and the natural systems. Ecology and international law provide us today a new mechanism to shape global environments. This combination is likely to evolve sustainable development. Above all, it will help adaptation of human beings to different ecological systems including different cultures. It will yield unity in diversity of global life. The combination of law-and-science and an ecological approach will promote world harmony. Talking about paradigms, Thomas Kuhn says in his eminent treatise, *The Structure of Scientific Revolution* that "Each (paradigm) produced a consequent shift in the problems available for scientific scrutiny and in the standards by which the profession determined what should count as an admissible problem or as a legitimate problem solution. And each transformed the scientific imagination in ways that we shall ultimately need to describe as a transformation of the world within which scientific work was done. Such changes, together with the controversies that accompany them, are the defining characteristics of scientific revolutions."[31]

The world may therefore by witnessing a scientific revolution which involves the synthesis of international law with global science providing a biologist view of the world which view is enacted and strengthened by the UN Declaration of 1972, and the UN World Charter for Nature of 1982, adopted in India as well. It is paradigm for world harmony, and harmony with nature. As Einstein has said in his famed address on the quest for scientific research:

"The longing to behold this pre-established harmony is the source of the inexhaustible patience[32] and perseverance with which Planck has devoted him to the most general problems of our science, refusing to let him be diverted to more profitable and more easily attained ends."[33]

To shape a creative life on this planet, it therefore becomes necessary to provide harmony between man made laws and the laws of nature, which is possible by a creative synthesis of law and science.[34]

Notes

1 *See,* Saligram Bhatt, *Environment Protection and Sustainable Development*, APH Publishing, 2004, p. 133, and Paper presented in 1996 to Indian Social Science Congress, Santiniketan.

2. Rabindranath Tagore, *Sadhna: The Realisation of Life,* Lectures in Harvard University, 1913, 1979 Edition, p. 50.

3. *See* Tagore, n. 1, p. 80.

4. Bae Nagchaudhuri and Bhatt, n. 2, p. 55.

5. *See* S. Bhatt, "Ecology and International Law", *Indian Journal of International Law,* Vol. 22, 1982, pp. 422-38.

6. *See* Albert Einstein, *Ideas and Opinions,* Calcutta, 1954, p. 226.

7. *Ibid.,* p. 135.

8. Cited by S. Bhatt, "Recent Developments in Outer Space: Law, Freedom and Responsibility after Lunar Landings", *Journal of Air Law of Commerce* (Dallas, Texas), Vol. 36, 1970, p. 268.

9. *Ibid.*

10. *See* B.M. Crook, Trans., New York, 1971.

11. See Ilya Prigogine and Isabella Stingers, *Order Out of Chaos: Man's New Dialogue with Nature,* N.Y., 1984, p. 292.
12. *Ibid.,* p. 136.
13. *Ibid.,* p. 293.
14. See Note on "The Nature of Reality: A Conversation between Dr Rabindranath Tagore and Professor Albert Einstein", in Tagore Reader, Amiya Chakravorty, ed., N.Y., 1961.
15. *Ibid.*
16. For text of Declaration, see *International Environmental Law,* Najmul Arif complied, Lancers Books, New Delhi, 1996, pp. 7-14.
17. *See,* Saligram Bhatt, *Environment Protection and Sustainable Development,* APH Publishing, 2004, p. 137.
18. *Ibid.,* p. 293.
19. *Ibid.,* p. 138.
20. *See,* Margaret Mead, "Anthropology Today" in P. Albertson and M. Barnett, eds., *Managing. The Planet,* 1972, p. 188.
21. *See,* S. Bhatt, n. 5, p. 428.
22. *Ibid.,* p. 139.
23. *See,* Victor Ferkiss, *The Future of Technological Civilisation,* N.Y., 1974, p. 206.
24. *Ibid.,* p. 207.
25. *Ibid.,* p. 303.
26. *See* text of World Charter for Nature in n. 12, pp. 15-20.
27. *Ibid.,* p.141.
28. *See* text in B. Desai, ed. *Environment Laws of India,* Lancers Books, 1994, pp. 81-94.
29. *Ibid.,* p. 142.
30. *See,* Thomas S. Kuhn, *The Structure of Scientific Revolutions,* London, 1962, p. 6.
31. *Ibid.,* p. 143.
32. A. Einstein, n. 6, p. 227.
33. *Ibid.,* p. 144.
34. Saxena, G., Clark, G., T. and Ilbery, B.(2007), Conceptualising Integrated Rural Tourism, Tourism Geographies, 9(4), pp. 347-370.

References

Albert Einstein (1954). *Ideas and Opinions,* Calcutta, p. 226.

Amiya Chakravorty (1961). "The Nature of Reality: A Conversation between Dr Rabindranath Tagore and Professor Albert Einstein", in Tagore Reader, ed., N.Y.

B. Desai (1994), ed. *Environment Laws of India,* Lancers Books, pp. 81-94.

B.M. Crook, Trans., New York, 1971.

Ilya Prigogine and Isabella Stingers (1984), Order Out of Chaos: Man's New Dialogue with Nature, N.Y., p. 292.

International Environmental Law (1996), Najmul Arif complied, Lancers Books, New Delhi, pp. 7-14.

Margaret Mead (1972), "Anthropology Today" in P. Albertson and M. Barnett, eds., *Managing. The Planet,* p.188.

Rabindranath Tagore (1913), *Sadhna: The Realisation of Life,* Lectures in Harvard University, 1979 Edition, p. 50.

S. Bhatt (1970). "Recent Developments in Outer Space: Law, Freedom and Responsibility after Lunar Landings", *Journal of Air Law of Commerce* (Dallas, Texas), Vol. 36, p. 268.

S. Bhatt (1982), "Ecology and International Law", Indian Journal of International Law, Vol. 22, pp. 422-38.

Saligram Bhatt (2004), *Environment Protection and Sustainable Development,* APH Publishing, 2004, p. 133, and Paper presented in 1996 to Indian Social Science Congress, Santinikitan.

Saligram Bhatt (2004), *Environment Protection and Sustainable Development,* APH Publishing, p. 137.

Thomas S. Kuhn (1962), *The Structure of Scientific Revolutions,* London, p. 6.

Victor Ferkiss (1974), *The Future of Technological Civilsation,* N.Y., p. 206.

World Charter for Nature in n. 12, pp. 15-20.

14

Plausible Linkage between Corporate Social Responsibility and Sustainable Tourism: A Qualitative Study of Tourism Business Units in Himachal Pradesh

Arun Sharma

Introduction

Corporate Social Responsibility (CSR) is a management concept whereby companies integrate social and environmental concerns in their business operations and interactions with their stakeholders. CSR is generally understood as being the way through which a company achieves a balance of economic, environmental and social imperatives, while at the same time addressing the expectations of shareholders and stakeholders. Any business unit that implements a CSR concept, can bring along a variety of competitive advantages, such as enhanced access to capital and markets, increased sales and profits, operational cost savings, improved productivity and quality, efficient human resource base, improved brand image and reputation, enhanced customer loyalty, better decision-making and risk management processes. Promoting the uptake of CSR amongst tourism enterprises requires approaches that fit the respective needs and capacities of these businesses, and do not adversely affect their economic viability. In developing countries, tourism is seen as a viable option for economic growth, but current unsustainable tourism practices in such countries can harm the health and well-being of the environment, community and tourism itself. Tourism industries often create negative impacts on the environment, society, culture, and sometimes even on the economy. However, few countries are using economic, regulatory or institutional policy instruments for tourism management (Logar, 2010). In most industries, corporate social responsibility (CSR) standards and practices have been developed by the private sector to respond to external pressure. In tourism, however, the use of codes of conduct and certification is not widespread and is not based as yet upon agreed international standards.

It is difficult to make generalisations about CSR without first examining the context in which sustainable tourism operates, its demands and also assessing the numerous certification schemes, codes of conduct and best practices within the industry. In 1988, the United Nations World Tourism Organisation (UNWTO) defined sustainable tourism as "leading to management of all resources in such a way that economic, social and aesthetic needs can be fulfilled while maintaining cultural integrity, essential ecological processes, biological diversity and life support systems". Later in 1992, the 'Earth Summit' in Rio established the triple principles of environmental, economic and social sustainability. Since then, the principles of sustainable tourism have been adopted by the tourism industry worldwide. As per the sustainable tourism criteria in India (Nov., 2011), the tourism sector is based on its unique endowments of biodiversity, forests, rivers, and its rich culture and heritage.

The challenges in this sector lie in successfully preserving these in their original form, and making them accessible to domestic and international travellers, together with safeguarding the economic interest and heritage of local communities. The importance of Sustainable Tourism worldwide has increased significantly due to the impact of increased human activity on climate. Nevertheless, it is necessary that the negative impact of the tourism industry is not enlarged unrealistically. Full advantage can then be drawn from the potential of tourism for inclusive growth with livelihoods support to the poor, most disadvantaged, women and youth. This cannot be achieved unless tourism entities understand the concept of CSR and adopt sustainable tourism practices in every operation.

Rationale of Study

The flow of tourists to a destination directly depends upon a number of factors (as per expectation of tourist) out of which major factors are service, facilities available, safety and security at the destination. Governments have not yet reached consensus on common approaches to CSR with respect to sustainable tourism, which has meant that the "rules" are being set de facto by the companies embracing it, and these are mostly large Transnational Companies (TNCs). As a result, SMEs (small and medium enterprises), especially those in developing countries and countries in transition, find themselves confronted with approaches to CSR that are often very incompatible to their economic and social contexts. Therefore, this research aims at examining the linkage between CSR and sustainable tourism.

Research Objectives

- To highlight the importance of CSR in the tourism trade.
- To emphasise sustainable tourism in the state.
- To motivate the people for responsible tourism business practices in the tourism industry.

Literature Review

Tourism needs to take into account a holistic and comprehensive approach that balances tourism development with other activities. Tourism is made up of many sectors and is very fragmented, therefore effects and monitoring processes through one company or mechanism would be difficult. The supply chain of product to end user is not often controlled solely by one party or individual and different elements are often operated by multiple stakeholders. This therefore has led to difficulties in controlling elements of corporate social responsibility. The United Nations Industrial Development Organisation (UNIDO)s CSR programme is based on the Triple Bottom Line (TBL) approach which is used as a framework for measuring and reporting corporate performance against economic, social and environmental performance. The perspective taken is that for an organisation to be sustainable, it must be financially secure, minimise (or ideally eliminate) its negative environmental impacts and act in conformity with societal expectations. UNIDO's Key CSR issues are environmental management, eco-efficiency, responsible sourcing, stakeholder engagement, labour standards and working conditions, employee and community relations, social equity, gender balance, human rights, good governance, and anti-corruption measures. In its CSR Projects, UNIDO usually targets all the levels (micro, meso, macro). As per an international organisation KPMG (*Klynveld, Peat, Marwick, Goerdeler)* report on CSR in 2011, the concept of CSR in India is not new, the process though acclaimed recently, has been followed since ancient times. Philosophers like Kautilya from India and pre-Christian era philosophers in the West preached and promoted ethical principles while doing business. The idea was also supported by several religions where it has been intertwined with religious laws. "Zakaat", followed by Muslims, is donation from one's earnings which is specifically given to the poor and disadvantaged. Similarly, Hindus follow the principle of

"Dhramada" and Sikhs the "Daashaant". In the global context, the recent history goes back to the eighteenth century when in 1790s, England witnessed the first large scale consumer boycott over the issue of slave harvested sugar which finally forced importers to have free labour sourcing. In India, in the pre-independence era, the businesses which pioneered industrialisation along with fighting for independence also followed the idea. They put the idea into action by setting up charitable foundations, educational and healthcare institutions, and trusts for community development. The term CSR itself came in to common use in the early 1970s. By late 1990s, the concept was fully recognised; people and institutions across all sections of society started supporting it.

Table 1: The four Models of CSR (Arora and Puranik, 2004)

Model	*Focus*	*Champion*
Ethical	Voluntary commitment by companies to public welfare	M.K. Gandhi
Static	State ownership and legal requirements determine corporate responsibility	Jawahar Lal Nehru
Liberal	Corporate responsibilities limited to private owners (shareholders)	Milton Friedman
Stake-Holder	Companies respond to the needs of stakeholders- customers, employees, communities, etc.	R. Edward Freeman

This can be corroborated by the fact that while in 1977 less than half of the Fortune 500 firms even mentioned CSR in their annual reports, by the end of 1990, approximately 90 per cent Fortune 500 firms embraced CSR as an essential element in their organisational goals, and actively promoted their CSR activities in annual reports (Boli and Hartsuiker, 2001). As per "Corporate Responsibility in India Poll", a survey conducted by Tata Energy Research Institute (TERI), the evolution of CSR in India has followed a chronological evolution of four thinking approaches as shown above in Table 1.

Concept of Corporate Social Responsibility (CSR)

The totality of CSR can be best understood by three words: "corporate", "social", and "responsibility". In broad terms, CSR relates to responsibilities corporations have towards society within which they are based and operate, not denying the fact that the purview of CSR goes much beyond this. CSR is comprehended differently by different people. Some perceive it to be a commitment of a company to manage its various roles in society, as producer, employer, customer and citizen in a responsible manner, while for others it is synonymous with Corporate Responsibility (CR) or Corporate Citizenship or Social Action Programme (SAP). Of late, the term has also been started to link up with Triple Bottom Line Reporting (TBL) which essentially measures an enterprise's performance against economic, social and environmental indicators. Discourses on CSR suggest that many definitions of CSR exist within the business community, and CSR continues to be an evolving concept, with no single definition that is universally accepted. Philip Kotler and Nancy Lee (2005) define CSR as "a commitment to improve community well being through discretionary business practices and contributions of corporate resources", whereas Mallen Baker refers to CSR as "a way companies manage the business processes to produce an overall positive impact on society." According to World Business Council for Sustainable Development "Corporate Social Responsibility is the continuing commitment by business to behave ethically and contribute to economic development while improving the quality of life of the workforce and their families as well as of the local community and society at large".

Myths about CSR

In the absence of a universally accepted definition for CSR, there are some myths that surround the concept:

A. Businesses invest the money, therefore they decide the modus operandi of the CSR initiative. There is a notion that since businesses invest money in society, they are the ones who will be deciding upon the modus operandi of the CSR initiative. However, this is not true. CSR driven by the mandate of an enterprise alone may not generate desired results. Stakeholders must be involved from the onset in defining an initiative to make it successful. Corporate must not assume that they understand the needs of a community by taking them at face value; stakeholder's needs must be considered within the local context and culture.

B. Financial resources alone cannot meet CSR needs of an enterprise. In fact, financial resources are only part of the equation. Besides financial resources, it is equally or even more important for the CSR programmes to be well defined and well accompanied by adequate human resources if they are to meet the intended objectives.

C. CSR is interchangeable with corporate sponsorship, donation or other philanthropic activities. The focus of responsible business practices in the profit sector is to largely confined to community charity-based projects. While this may have been relevant for the historical context in the mid-90s when Carroll's definition was coined, the current thinking of CSR has moved beyond philanthropy to in fact encompass all internal and external segments of business operations: employees, market, environment and community.

Methodology

This research study is based on both extensive secondary research and a large number of key informant interviews. Firstly, a review of existing literature demand for sustainable tourism was conducted. Then supplementary interviews with ten managers (three hotels, three tour operators, three event managers and one airlines manager) were carried out to assess the demand for sustainable tourism. Companies approached to be interviewed included the famous tour operators, hoteliers, airline and destination management companies. From September 2012- September 2013, the researcher had the arrangements to interview these key people through the relationship with his previous employer and his friends' through snowball or chain sampling method (Babbie, 2002: 179; Patton, 2002: 237). For the purpose of studying the linkage between Corporate Social Responsibility and sustainable tourism, the interview sessions were conducted through different theme based questions (see annexure 1). Suggestions and conclusion are drawn on the basis of interpretations of selected content.

CSR in Context of Sustainable Development of Tourism

Sustainable development has been defined as development that meets the needs of present and host regions while protecting and enhancing opportunities for the future. Sustainable tourism requires a holistic, integrated perspective that takes into account all the industries and resources upon which tourism relies. The set of criteria or principles that define the conditions for its achievement comprises: protect and conserve sustainable resources, be a multi-stakeholder approach, be environmentally responsible, maintain the well-being and involvement of the local population or host, provide meaningful and fairly remunerated employment for the host population, have economic benefit with a long-term view as well as a triple-bottom line approach (environmental, social and economic). Also it should be equitable, government must play a leadership role (e.g., impose a "greater good" approach) and obtain optimum guest satisfaction by educating the tourists about environmental and social concerns. In a developing tourist destination context, where legislation to protect community interests and the environment is either weak or often violated, CSR plays a less prominent role. Accountability has to precede any CSR. Human rights and the rights to livelihood of the local people need to be respected. However, while in all other sectors child labour is decreasing, there has been a marginal increase in child labour in tourism. This is the need of the hour that we need strong laws along with their proper implementation. The companies should also be scrutinised, in case there are land issues, labour issues, etc. Simion, Mazilu, Pătruþescu, and Ispas (2010) summarised the fundamental indicators of sustainable tourism as displayed in Table 2.

Table 2: Fundamental indicators of sustainable tourism: Simion, Mazilu, Pătruþescu, Ispas (2010)

1. Site Protection	The category of the site's protection after the index of the International Union for the Preservation of Nature (IUCN)
2. Pressure	The number of tourists who visit the site (year/month with maximum influx)
3. Intensity of use	The intensity of use during peak periods (the number of people and per hectare)
4. Social impact	The report tourists/residents (during the peak period, but also during the rest of the period)
5. Development control	The existence of a method of study of the environment or specific controls on the planning method of the area and the density of use
6. Waste management	Ratio of treated wastewater of the site (additional indicators may lead to structural limitations of other site infrastructure capacity, such as the water supply)
7. Planning process	The existence of a methodical plan for the tourist destination in question (with a component "tourism")
8. Fragile ecosystems	The number of rare species or endangered ones
9. Customer satisfaction	Visitor satisfaction (using a questionnaire)
10. Satisfaction of the local population	Satisfaction of the local population (using a questionnaire)
11. Contribution of tourism to local economy	How much tourism represents (%) in all the economic activity

CSR and Sustainable Tourism in Himachal Pradesh

Tourism is perceived as a fast growing segment worldwide and it requires the responsible attention of all the stakeholders and decision makers. Himachal Pradesh, a hilly state of India, is made up of 12 districts with a total area of 55,673 sq km. As per Himachal Pradesh economic survey 2013, tourism in Himachal Pradesh has been recognised as one of the most important sectors of the economy as it is being realised as a major engine of growth for future. State is endowed with all the basic resources necessary for thriving tourism activity like geographical and cultural diversity, clean, peaceful and beautiful streams, sacred shrines, historic monuments and the friendly and hospitable people. The tourism industry in Himachal Pradesh has been given very high priority and the government has developed the appropriate infrastructure for its development, which includes the provision of public utility services, roads, communication network, airports, transport facilities, water supply and civic amenities etc. The state government has targeted development of tourism and civil aviation. At present 2,609 hotels having bed capacity of 59,585 are registered with the department up to December, 2012. The Government of India have approved a project amounting to 3.68 crore for the creation of Eco-tourism infrastructure in pre-identified eco-circuit. The departmental activities carried out at present are the maintenance of old heritage forest rest houses, development of trades and training, identification of local flora and fauna etc. In the field of publicity and promotion the department has established brand Himachal as an attractive tourist destination under the caption 'Unforgettable Himachal'. At present there are only three airports namely, Shimla, Kangra and Kullu. These are operational but very less/poor airline services are drawbacks for tourism in the state. There are 57 operational helipads and 12 new helipads are also in offing. The State government has decided to introduce heli-taxi services in the State to improve connectivity and open up remote and tribal areas to the tourists. Availability of natural resources makes the state suitable for investments in sectors such as tourism, agricultural, horticulture, hydro power and cement industries. The government has a very strict action plan for CSR; recently 34 hotels have been closed at Manali those were violating the rules and damaging the ecosystem. Moreover, the use of plastic, smoking, mining of natural resources is completely banned in the state.

Demand for Sustainable Tourism

Every year tourists from worldwide visit the beautiful valley of Himachal Pradesh popularly called "Dev bhoomi" in the Himalayas, with numerous ancient villages where the architecture is in stone and timber, friendly people follow rich traditional customs everyday, magnificent mountains and scenic beauty is present all-round. In order to safeguard one of the biggest asset to tourism (cultural heritage, old temples traditional houses with beautiful carvings, beautiful majestic mountains, dense forests, flowing river) it is mandatory to make everybody responsible for tourism whether tourist or host or middleman. The destinations like Shimla, Manali, Mecklodganj are over their carrying capacity. Due to unsustainable (business practices, management of tourism resourses and strict implementation of laws) the crime rates (especially robbery, rape, prostitution) are increasing, destinations are facing overcrowding. As a result pollution is increasing which is spoiling the environment as well as the destination's image in the mind of tourists. Finally the heritage (tangible and intangible) of the state is dying an unnatural death which demands an immediate responsible action which is possible only once everybody understands their responsibilities.

Demand for CSR within Tourism

Within the tourism industry it is generally agreed that there are increasing overall societal and environmental concerns, and that this will increase the demand for more sustainable destinations and travel preferences. These will increase the pressure for destination management policies and tour operator responsibility. The destinations which were the result of overbuilding, are expected to face severe decline as consumers look for more attractive destinations that feature a clean environment and well preserved natural and cultural attractions. Another trend affecting sustainable tourism is health and wellness. Active or adventure holidays, wellness and spa products and snow destinations are likely to increase in popularity.

Results and Discussion

Based on the interviews conducted, it is clear that guidelines alone are not strong enough to overcome the short-term profit motive of many operators, governments and destinations. At the same time, organisations have framed excellent documents as their CSR initiatives but ground reality is far away as there is no proper implementation of the same. Most of the business heads are aware about the concept of CSR and strongly believe that this approach is useful for facilitating sustainable tourism. This research emphasised an evident demand for sustainable tourism in Himachal Pradesh as there are much more informal/unregistered agents those involved in various unethical practices like (Foreign exchange in black, duping the tourists by misleading them, polluting the business environment as well as natural beauty, supplying drugs to the tourists leading to various crimes etc) therefore creating a big threat to the whole tourism industry in the state. As per the words of a tour operator we have special deals for the people with disabilities as our CSR initiatives. It is observed that even the well educated managers only relate the concept of CSR with society, completely forgetting other aspects (environment and economy). It is difficult to implement the awareness programme at ground level as people are busy with their own schedule. The Tourism Industry may not be able to completely implement CSR until everybody has become aware and equally responsible for each and every tourism activity, which is possible only through education. More research is needed to determine how the product can be shifted to include sustainability. If the consumer and the industry are driven by price then there is a need to re-think the strategy of how to include sustainability within current cost structures.

Practical implications of this research can be recapitulated as follows: Governments should focus their capacity-building efforts on suppliers, using such methods as legislated compliance (e.g., environmental, reputation and business probity), ensuring that resources are available for training and learning by suppliers and, where needed, fill resource gaps. Government must encourage public-private partnerships of training for environmental and social awareness and mitigation strategies as well as offering incentives and reporting guidelines to the tourism sector distributed through industry associations. Support training and the sharing of best practices. Decision makers should encourage industry associations to make adherence to sustainable or responsible tourism policies a condition of membership and to report on progress. Encourage CSR reporting from tour operators, transporters, hotels, and destinations themselves so that they can understand the impact they themselves are having. Reporting will also provide measurable criteria by which companies and destinations can be compared.

Table3: Plausible Linkage between Tourism and CSR

CSR Core Areas	*Facilitators*	*Benefits*
Market Place	Consumers and shareholders	Motivated to invest in projects
Work place	Unions and employees	Please to work for long time
Environment	Government and NGO's	Build positive destination image
Society	Local community	All round social development
Ethical Business	Business units	Strong economy

Suggestions

As Himachal Pradesh is reviewing the state tourism policy of 2005 with technical assistance from the World Bank to give more emphasis to sustainable tourism development in the state. All-round efforts are being made to protect this valley from the adverse effect of tourism and the negative approach brought on by modernity. Everyone in the state of Himachal and nearby areas should combine their joint efforts in the fields of tourism and agriculture to make everything sustainable. Whereas the decision makers need to ensure strict implementation of actions for minimising deforestation and air pollution, by using more of solar energy, renovation of old buildings for guesthouses and new ones to be built on old traditional style. All rubbish to be collected and disposed in an organised manner, efforts should be to reduce pollution created by vehicles as well as public transport system to be supported. There should be demarcation of protected areas to reduce the impact of tourism on this area. Working conditions to be created for local people to generate more jobs which are eco-friendly and give a fair livelihood. More of local products to be used; the promotion of local cuisine at all eating-places will add feathers to the caps of tourism. Special incentives should be given to the farmers for eco-friendly agricultural practices and use of organic materials. Government must come up with strategic tourism planning as well as clear roles and objectives. Therefore, focusing on public-private partnership to forward the CSR agenda should have a greater overall positive impact and advance sustainable tourism in the industry. In order to enhance sustainable tourism there is a need to focus on elements of the tourism industry which can affect a greater number of products and businesses and contribute environmentally, socially and economically. Moreover, Himachal Tourism must keep in mind the international standards and imposed social and environmental criteria to foreign investors by seeing not only short-term economic gains but a long-term, holistic and sustainable tourism development. Finally, everybody in the state should be motivated to protect the tourism resources (specially heritage, nature and culture) through awareness programmes on a regular basis in close cooperation with the institutions.

Need of the Hour

Labour standards as part of sustainable tourism: The major labour issues which affect the tourism industry include women's rights, fair wages, long working hours, qualification and skills requirements for employees, inability to join trade unions, importing of labour and displacement of traditional employment to benefit from tourism dollars. Tourism workers often do not earn a living wage and are dependent on tips and service charges. Many workers have temporary contracts or none at all, work long hours and are employed in low skilled areas such as waitressing and/or house cleaning.

Customer Motivation: Customers' decisions are often dominated by price. Price, accommodation quality and personal security rank as the most important considerations of tourism. Consumers are susceptible to health and safety issues, however, with cleanliness and quality being major factors in their destination choice. From existing research and interviews with tourism business unit heads and other experts, it can be concluded that consumers would change their destination choice as a result of bad press about health (e.g. spoiled destinations) or safety issues, but not for lack of environmental or social responsibility on the part of suppliers.

Environmental safety: Every tourism activity has a strong impact on the environment; therefore, we need to further develop the concept of an international certification label for the travel and tourism industry that is inclusive (environmental, social, cultural etc.), affordable, monitored, and reported. In order to achieve more sustainable forms of tourism, it needs to move away from voluntary measures towards reporting where progress can be measured and buyers and suppliers held accountable for their actions.

Active Government participation: CSR could help with a number of issues facing tourism with regard to promoting sustainable tourism practices, however, industry must see government involvement and support if they are to increase their own involvements in CSR. There is a need for governments to step up to the challenge of ensuring more sustainable forms of tourism will be supported and to reassure investors and players in the tourism sector that government will support and encourage sustainable tourism management and development.

Conclusion

The present scenario is an alarming stage for whole world to care for the resources available on earth. This is only possible if everybody will understand his/her own responsibility and become equally responsible for every business practice. More and more firms are registering everyday for manufacturing and distributing the new products and services, the businessmen hardly bothers about their CSR - corporate social responsibility. The ultimate aim of these people is simply to earn money any how. As a result of unsustainable utilisation of resources' our natural resources' are decaying and our cultural resources' are dying an unnatural death. CSR reporting means a company is more transparent and accountable to external stakeholders, enabling investors to avoid risk and consumers to support more sustainable businesses, therefore having a multiplier effect. Whereas sustainable tourism implies minimising the negative and maximising the positive effects of all forms and activities of tourism on: environment, local communities, heritage (cultural, natural, built, oral, intangible) and inclusive economic growth. In the condition of higher living standards, people tend to spend a lot of money for entertainment and travel besides their basic needs for eating, clothing, and living). Sustainable tourism can help overcome many of the negative impacts associated with tourism development once everybody either industry or individuals understand their responsibility of safeguarding the society, culture, heritage, environment, economy and all the resources' for tourism. Finally the active involvement, joint research as well smooth coordination of industry, academia and government will lead the destinations to becoming sustainable and everybody will observe a real time CSR implementation.

References

Arora, B. and Puranik, R. (2004), "A review of corporate social responsibility in India", Development, Vol. 47 No. 3, pp. 93-100.

Simion, D., Mazilu, M., Patrutescu, M., and Ispas, R. (2010). *The Economic and Social*

Contribution of Tourism from the Sustainable Development Point of View. Proceedings of the 5th WSEAS International Conference on Economy and Management Transformation (Volume I).

Babbie, E. (2002). *The Basics of Social Research* – Second Edition. California: Wadsworth.

Erku°-Öztürk, H., and Eraydýn, A. (2010). Environmental governance for sustainable tourism development: Collaborative networks and organisation building in the Antalya tourism region. *Tourism Management*, Vol. 31 No. 1, pp. 113-124. http://dx.doi.org/10.1016/j.tourman. 2009.01. 002

Logar, I. (2010). Sustainable tourism management in Crikvenica, Croatia: An assessment of policy instruments. *Tourism Management*, Vol. 31 No. 1, pp. 125-135. http://dx.doi.org/10.1016/j.tourman.2009.02.005

Miller, G., Rathouse, K., Scarles, C., Holmes, K., and Tribe, J. (2010). Public understanding of sustainable tourism. *Annals of Tourism Research*, Vol. 37 No. 3, pp. 627-645. http://dx.doi.org/10.1016/j.annals.2009.12.002

Patton, M.Q. (2002). *Qualitative evaluation and research methods* (3rd ed.). Thousand Oaks, CA: Sage Publications, Inc.

Web resources

http://thepartneringinitiative.org/w/wp-content/uploads/2012/04/BizNGO_India.pdf

http://www.wbiworldconpro.com/uploads/canada-conference 2013/management/1370168444_430-Sonam.pdf

www.grin.com/en/e-book/137651

www.mallenbaker.net

www.wbcsd.org

http://www.unido.org/

http://www.tourism-review.com/travel-tourism-magazine-csr-in-tourism-ongoing-discussion-article1280#FtPIFZyYdh589zBA.99

http://www.kpmg.com

*www.**unido**.org/what-we-do/trade/csr/what-is-csr.htmlý*

*www.in.kpmg.com/pdf/**csr**_whitepaper.pdfý*

15

Rural Tourism as a Medium for Local Development in Himachal Pradesh:

The Example of Villages around Dharamshala (Kangra)

Amit Katoch and Dr Prashant Kumar Gautam

Introduction

Tourism is one of the leading and top growing industries in the world. It provides work for millions of people and generates nine per cent of the worldwide GDP. In more than 150 countries, tourism is one of the five pinnacle export earners, and in 60 it is the number one export. It accounts to six per cent of the world's exports amounting to US$ 1.3 trillion and generates one in eleven jobs. In India, too, tourism has shown an impressive growth. It contributes 6.23 per cent to the national GDP (WTTC) and provides 7.9 per cent of the total employment in India (Ministry of Tourism, Government of India). According to the World

Tourism Organisation, by the year 2020, it is expected that India will become the leader in the tourism industry in South Asia, with about 8.9 million arrivals.

The inclinations of the world market, the user needs, the revision of opinion concerning what describes life quality and principal goods, the development of ecological awareness and the understanding of universal tourist experience accrued throughout the entire years, the alteration of the policies and strategies that have been implemented in the field of tourism up to the present all have contributed to the evolution and expansion of new niches in tourism. Now, alternative forms of tourism are being developed keeping in view the consciousness man has developed over the years with regard to the environment, minimising the negative impacts of tourism and avoiding the hectic, complex monotonous routine ways which have resulted due to modernisation, globalisation and industrialisation.

Rural tourism was an alternative form of tourism which developed throughout the world to support the rural economies of regions which were far off, inaccessible, non-industrialised and largely agrarian. It is a tourism which was alternative to mass tourism. This novel type of tourism started to expand after the commencement of rural mass departure to urban areas during the Industrial Revolution. And a need was felt to create employment opportunities in rural areas, so that these areas could also develop hand in hand with urban areas. Agriculture is the mainstay activity in rural areas and the majority of people is dependent on it. But, there has been continuous slowdown in agriculture throughout the world, so, apart from diversification of agriculture, a need was also felt to focus on vocational activities which could benefit the rural population socially and economically. Rural spaces should no longer be seen as purely associated with agriculture production but seen as locations for the stimulation of new socio-economic activities incorporating tourism, leisure, hospitality, food production and consumption and e-commerce.

Rural tourism is also seen as a way to get disadvantaged rural areas out of crisis and to provide solutions that tourism could provide to the problems of rural less-favoured areas (Sharpley, 2002; Sarasa, 2001). Tourism has been studied for its economic (Martin and Uysal, 1990; Mathieson and Wall, 1982), environmental (Farrell and Runyan, 1991), cultural (Chambers, 1997; Smith, 1989), and social (Milman and Pizam, 1987; Wyllie, 2000) impact. Rural tourism strategies in various countries have in common that they are a major growth area that can be used to boost local communities, and aid the seasonal and geographic spread of tourism (Richards, 1996). Tourism also contributes to the local community by improving the standard of living, providing employment opportunities, providing investment for the development of infrastructures and as a mean of financial and social development. (Smith and Krannich, 1998; Verbole, 2000; Keller, 2002; Andriotis, 2001). But apart from the affirmative effects, tourism at times also has a negative side such as the imitation of foreign models by the local community, the commercialisation of human interactions, the transformation of regions of exceptional natural beauty into over satiated urban regions, the pollution of the surroundings, the pessimistic cultural changes, etc, (Kokkosis, 2001; Kokkosis and Tsartas, 2001; Spilanis, 2000). Tourism is often criticised for its evil or monstrous effects (Romeril, 1985; Vanhove, 1997) which result in demolition of tourist regions and their cultural fabric.

The three villages Dharmkot, Satovari and Barnet have been selected for the qualitative research. The study area lies in the lap of Dhauladhar range and is marked by steep mountain ridges and valleys.

Objectives of Research

The broad objectives of the research study are as follows:

- To inspect the rural tourism resources of the three villages (Satovari, Barnet and Dharmkot) around Dharamshala for rural tourism.

- To identify the rural population's understanding of the rural tourism development and its consequent benefits.
- To examine the willingness of the communities to participate in rural tourism.

Research Methodology

This study is exploratory and qualitative in nature and is based on the experience of the researcher after visiting the three villages (Satovari, Barnet and Dharmkot) around Dharamshala for rural tourism. The study is ethnographic in nature aimed at exploring the potential of rural tourism phenomena in three villages and exploring it as a means of local development. The participant observation has been done which is overt observation. The information has been gathered after interacting with the villagers informally; knowing their understanding about rural tourism and their willingness to participate in it. The information provided in this research study is fully reliable, vigorous, logical and reliable. The author has tried to compile a comprehensive and complete view of villagers by continuously interacting with them.

Limitations of the Study

The study has been carried through overt observation (Participant Observation Type) and two days each has been spent by the researcher at each village. One of the major drawbacks with this type of research is that it may be affected by Observer effect, where the conduct of folks under study may change due to the presence of the researcher.

Advantages of the Study

The main advantages of the use of overt observation are that:

- It may lead to evasion of nuisance of ethics in that the group are conscious of the researcher's function.

- The grouping is examined in its standard surroundings and data can be openly recorded.
- Problems of 'going native' are avoided.
- The researcher gives the viewpoint after having experience in natural setting of the three villages.

Rural Tourism in India

In India, the scheme of rural tourism was launched in 2002-03, not merely keeping in mind the economic objectives, but also the social, cultural and ecological aspects of the rural destination. The Rural Tourism project has also been taken up with United Nations Development Programme (UNDP) under the Ministry's Endogenous Tourism Project in 2003 to support community and village-based tourism in India. The five broad objectives of this initiative were to do capacity building at the local level, try out with location-specific models of community tourism enterprise, put together strong community-private ventures, maintain pioneering and promising rural tourism projects and provide inputs to national and state tourism policy.

Till January 2012, rural tourism projects at 183 sites have been sanctioned in India and 52 rural sites have been commissioned (June, 2011). Also, this segment of Indian Tourism has been winning accolades in the international arena. For example, the rural tourism project at Hodka village in Kutch district of Gujarat have received PATA award in 2010 for Heritage category and CNBC Awaaz Travel Award in 2008 for Best Tourism Income Generating Community. Also, Village Naggar, District Kullu, Himachal Pradesh has received PATA award in 2008 for Demonstrating Women Empowerment at its best.

In the twelfth five year plan (2012-2017), in order to develop rural tourism, emphasis has been given on cluster approach i.e. Rural Tourism Clusters (RTCs) rather than the single village approach. For the development of rural tourism clusters, a three phase process has been adopted. The first phase involves selection of site by national level consultant of the Ministry of Tourism in consultation with state government and travel trade. The second phase involves review of the DPR by Ministry of Tourism through independent agencies and sanction of central financial assistance by the Ministry of Tourism for approved projects. The third phase involves execution of the rural tourism cluster project. For a cluster of six villages a central financial assistance of 11 crore is recommended for physical infrastructure and capacity building. For each village a amount of Rupees 1.5 crore is allocated, keeping Rupees two crore for common facilities/activities in each cluster.

Rural Tourism in Himachal Pradesh

Himachal Pradesh is one of the states in India which has got great diversity in terms of travel and tourism. It offers a colourful, extravagant, graceful, and diverse aspect of her personality to each traveller. Himachal Pradesh provides varied kinds of tourism options such as Adventure Tourism, Religious Tourism, Rural Tourism, Sustainable Tourism, Eco-Tourism, Green Tourism, Golf Tourism, Nature Tourism, Medical Tourism apart from Cultural and Heritage Tourism. Himachal Pradesh is a land which is bequeathed with natural splendour at its best – picturesque locations; snow capped mountains, luxuriant green valleys, a cool climate and hospitable people. Himachal Pradesh has got immense tourism potential.

The State government's tourism policy is now diversifying tourism to regions which are novel and have tourism potential. That is why efforts are being made to promote rural tourism and diversify tourists to the countryside or new areas and decongest the over saturated tourist destinations. The State received over 150 lakh tourists (2012), from which 4.85 lakh was foreign tourists. On the whole the regime is committed to have sustainable tourism with special importance on diversification, accessibility and job creations.

Rural tourism is now the new buzz word for the development of tourism in Himachal Pradesh. The concept of Atithi Devo Bhava has been redefined by the Government of Himachal Pradesh by steering the new scheme of "Har Gaon Ki Kahani"- the story of every village. And this tourism scheme was carefully prepared in order to persuade more tourists in the rustic areas of the state. The Himachal Tourism Department has recognised 12 villages to be developed for promoting Rural Tourism. And a total budget outlay of Rs 20243.92 crore has been declared for this purpose. Through the ground-breaking scheme of 'Har Gaon Ki Kahani', rural infrastructure would be developed in Himachali hamlets for the endorsement of rural tourism. In this programme there will be a contribution of all government departments as well as the local community. This will give a major boost to the development of the rural areas besides promoting the local handicrafts, indigenous products and cultural activities. The 'Har Gaon Ki Kahani' scheme was first launched in 2010 under which the Tourism Department had asked villagers to come up with popular stories related to their villages for attracting tourists. As per the plan one village from each district was selected such as Shamsher in Kullu, Salasi in Bilaspur, Bela in Hamirpur, Sangrah in Sirmour, Baggi in Mandi, Saho in Chamba, Nerti in Kangra, Udaipur in Lahaul and Spiti, Brua in Kinnaur, Baniya Devi in Solan, Hewan in Shimla and Nari in Una.

Rural Tourism Resources of the Villages Selected

The three villages (Satovari, Barnet and Dharmkot) are located on the vicinity of the Dharamshala town, which itself is a main hub of tourism activity. And renowned throughout the world for its picturesque beauty and is a seat of the Tibetan government in exile. It is the winter capital of the state of Himachal Pradesh and recently it was in news for its cricket stadium.

The three villages selected for the study have great potential for rural tourism. The village Dharmkot is a small hill village on the crest of a hill above McLeod Ganj, near Dharamshala. It is located at a distance of 14 km at an altitude of 2100 m. Dharmkot is an gorgeous village that presents a extensive sight of the Kangra valley and the Dhauladhar ranges. There are a number of Ghaddi families present here. Also, there are a number of eateries and guest houses flocked by a large number of foreigners. Lots of foreigners have made Dharmkot their home and have taken fields and houses from local Indians on rent. It is also branded as a hippie colony, where Hebrew is spoken most commonly. There are also a large number of local meditation centres. Also, Dharmkot acts as the starting place for a large number of trekking routes such as Triund, Ilaqua. Also temple of Galu Devi temple and Bhagsu Nag temple are located on the surroundings of this village. This village is also very famous for Pizza which is made on a traditional base. The most famous restaurant for Pizzas is Pizzeria which is owned by a Gaddi family. The speciality of this pizza is that it is made on a traditional base made at home and cooked on a Chula (traditional wood stove).

Satovari is also a small picturesque village located North West and at an approximately 14 km of the Dharamshala town at an elevation of 1729 m. This village also has number of tourist resources such as picturesque view of Kangra valley and Dhauladhar ranges; Dull Lake; lush green pine forests; flora and fauna ; tribal culture of Ghaddi's; Trekking; Hiking etc.

Barnet is one of the most beautiful village present in the surrounding of Dharamshala at an distance of 17 km away having an altitude of 1458 m. The majority of houses present here have a vernacular architecture made of mud bricks with the roof made of slates and present in the mid of the fields. Barnet is located 3 km away from Satovari and gradually descends. The village, too, is inhabited by the

Gaddi Tribe and the main occupation of the rural people is agriculture. The researcher has revealed ample scope for rural tourism in the three villages selected for rural tourism. The inventory of attraction clearly demonstrates the vast potential available for rural tourism.

Table 2: Elements of Tourism product present in the three villages

Type of attract-tion	*Resources*	*Dharmkot*	*Satovari*	*Barnet*
Natural attraction	Scenic Beauty/ Mountains/ River/Rivulet/ Fields/Waterfall/Lake/Forest/ Flora/Fauna/ Protected national park/ Sanctuaries/ Sunset / sunrise view/ Landforms/ Unique Geology site	Present	Present	Present
Cultural attraction	Culture/Folklore/ Handicraft/ Cuisine / Music Language/ Historical monument/ Vernacular Architecture/ Cultural landscape/ Temple Religion	Present	Present	Present
Activity	Mountaineering/ hiking/trekking/Swimming/ Camping / Paragliding potential	Present	Present	Present
Events/ festivals		Present	Present	Present

Elements of Tourism product	*Dharmkot*	*Satovari*	*Barnet*
Accommodation	Present	Present	-
Accessibility	Present	Present	Present
Attraction	Present	Present	Present
Activities	Present	Present	Present
Basic amenities	Present	Present	Present

Resident Profile: Agriculture is the main occupation of the people in the two villages i.e. Barnet and Satovari, but in the case of Dharmkot rural people are also involved in guest houses, small restaurants and adventure activities. The majority of the residents from which researcher interacted were higher secondary and very few were graduates and postgraduates.

Rural Population Understanding of the Rural Tourism, Rural Development and Rural Participation in Tourism

The rural people present in the three villages had a clear understanding and awareness with regard to tourism. But, however, their understanding with regard to rural tourism was not very well developed. They had a lot of confusion. Also, they were not aware of the tourism policies at state and central level. Some of the residents were aware of the Home Stay scheme which was launched by the government in 2008 to augment the rural areas in terms of accommodation and to provide clean, comfortable and affordable supplementary accommodation to tourists in rural areas. But overall the residents of the three villages were aware of the benefits of tourism for the local community in terms of employment, rise in income level, local development, and high quality of life. On contrary, they were not worried much about the ill effects of tourism such as overcrowding, congestion, inflation of goods and services, crime, overdevelopment, traffic congestion, pressure on local resources, value of the real estate etc. A few individuals, however, voiced their concern over the environmental, social and cultural issues. The researcher observed that the residents of the three villages especially Barnet and Satovari was that still people need a lot of awareness about rural tourism and the pros and cons associated with it.

Findings and Conclusions

The majority of rural population of the three villages is aware about tourism and the benefits associated with it;

Table 3: Opinion of the Rural Community in the three villages' w.r.t. rural tourism and rural development

Area of opinion	*Sub- issues*	*Dharmkot*			*Satovari*			*Barnet*		
	Opinion	Yes (%)	Can't say (%)	No (%)	Yes (%)	Can't say (%)	No (%)	Yes (%)	Can't say (%)	No (%)
Tourism	Awareness of tourism	90	10	-	80	10	10	80	10	10
	Knew about rural tourism	30	40	30	25	15	60	15	20	65
	Government policies w.r.t. Rural Tourism	20	60	20	20	10	70	20	30	50
	Basis of tourism should be based on decisions of local community & community participation	80	10	10	80	10	10	90	10	-
	Sustainable development	80	10	10	85	10	5	80	10	10
Positive effect of Tourism	Employment	75	15	10	80	15	5	80	10	10
	Encourage investment in local community	70	15	15	60	10	20	65	15	20
	Enhancement of infrastructure	80	-	20	70	15	15	70	10	20
	Enhance quality of life	60	20	20	55	25	20	80	20	-
	Development of the village	80	10	10	70	10	20	75	15	10
	Development of the recreation facilities for locals	55	25	20	50	30	20	25	40	25

Area of opinion	*Sub- issues*	*Dharmkot*			*Satovari*			*Barnet*		
	Opinion	Yes (%)	Can't say (%)	No (%)	Yes (%)	Can't say (%)	No (%)	Yes (%)	Can't say (%)	No (%)
Negative effect of Tourism	Destruction of environment	30	20	50	35	15	50	35	10	55
	Congestion & overcrowding	35	5	60	25	15	60	30	10	60
	Burden on community services	25	10	65	20	20	60	20	15	65
	Crime	20	10	70	20	20	60	25	5	70
	Higher taxes	35	15	50	25	15	60	35	5	55
	Overdevelopment	25	25	50	20	10	70	30	10	60
	Inflation	30	20	50	30	10	60	25	20	55
	Increase in the cost of Land	60	10	30	25	25	50	30	20	50

Table 4: Opinion of the Rural Community in the three villages w.r.t. their willingness in rural tourism

Area of opinion	*Sub- issues*	*Dharmkot*			*Satovari*			*Barnet*		
	Opinion	Ye s (%)	Can't say (%)	No (%)	yes	Can't say (%)	No (%)	Ye s (%)	Can't say (%)	No (%)
Willingness to involve in Rural tourism	Rural tourism will lead to overall well-being of village	80	10	10	70	20	10	60	20	10
	It will provide new opportunities	75	15	10	65	15	20	60	10	30

however, they have little understanding about rural tourism and rural tourism policy implemented by the government (State as well as Central). Also, they are very receptive about the benefits of tourism, while not having a very clear view of the negative aspects of tourism. The territorial diagnoses of the three villages clearly helps us to understand the potential of tourism and assets associated with it. And to reveal the overall perception of the local community to involve in rural tourism.

But still the local community is unaware about the basic concept of rural tourism. They do not have a clear understanding about what rural tourism is and that what is the role of the local community.

It clearly underlines the importance that if we want to develop rural tourism in these villages, a rural tourism awareness campaign should be launched prior to rural tourism activity, so that sustainable development occurs and that negative impacts with regard to economic, social and ecological factors could be avoided.

Notes

1. Sharpley R. (2002) Rural tourism and the challenge of tourism diversification: the case of Cyprus. *Tourism Management*, Vol. 23, No. 3, pp. 233-244.
2. Andres Sarasa, J.L., (2001) El désafío del turismo en espacio rural. Proceedings

   from IV Congreso Universidad y Empresa, Valencia, Spain, 2001.
3. Martin S. and M. Uysal (1990). An examination of the relationship between carrying capacity and the tourism lifecycle: Management and policy implications. Journal of Environmental Management, Vol. 31, pp. 327-333.
4. Mathieson A. and Wall G. (1982). Tourism: Economic, Physical, and Social Impacts. McAdam D., J. McCarthy and M. N. Zald eds. New York: Longman.

5. Farrell H. and D. Runyan (1991). Ecology and Tourism. Annals of Tourism Research,Vol. 18, pp. 26–40.
6. Chambers R. (1997). Whose Reality Counts? Putting the last first. Bath, England, The Bath Press, pp. 89-91.
7. Smith V. (ed.) (1989). Hosts and Guests: The Anthropology of Tourism. Philadelphia: University of Pennsylvania Press.
8. Milman. A.. and A. Pizam (1987). Social Impacts of Tourism on Central Florida. *Annals of Tourism Research*, Vol. 15, pp.191–204.
9. Smith D. and Krannich S. (1998). Tourism Dependence and Resident Attitudes. *Annals of Tourism Research*, Vol. 25, No 4, pp. 783-802.
10. Verbole A. (2000). Actors, Discourses and Interfaces of Rural Tourism Development at the Local Community Level in Slovenia: Social and Political Dimensions of the Rural Tourism Development Process. *Journal of Sustainable Tourism*, Vol. 8, No 6. pp. 479-490.
11. Romeril M. (1985). Tourism and the environment: towards a symbiotic relationship. *International Journal of Environmental Studies*, Vol. 25, No. 4, pp. 215-218.
12. Vanhove N. (1997). Mass tourism: Benefits and costs. In: Wahab S. and Pigram J. J.(eds): *Tourism Development and Growth - The Challenge of Sustainability*. London: Routledge, pp. 50-77.

References

Andriotis K. (2001). Tourism Planning and Development in Crete. Recent Tourism Policies and their Efficacy. *Journal of Sustainable Tourism*, Vol 9, No 4, pp. 298-316.

Andriotis K. (2002a). Local Authorities in Crete and the Development of Tourism. *The Journal of Tourism Studies*, Vol. 13, No 2, pp. 53-62.

Andriotis K. (2002b). Options in tourism development. Conscious versus conventional tourism. *Anatolia an International Journal of Tourism and Hospitality Research*, Vol.13, No 1, pp. 73-85.

Andriotis K. (2005). Community Groups Perceptions and Preferences to Tourism Development: Evidence from Crete. *Journal of Hospitality and Tourism Research*, Vol.29, No 1, pp. 67-90.

Bramwell B. (1994). Rural tourism and sustainable rural tourism. *Journal of Sustainable Tourism,* Vol. 2, No. 1-2, pp. 1-21.

Chambers R. (1997). Whose Reality Counts? Putting the last first. Bath, England, The Bath Press, pp. 89-91.

Farrell H. and D. Runyan (1991). Ecology and Tourism. *Annals of Tourism Research,* Vol. 18, pp. 26–40.

Fotiadis A. (2006). Cultural Interactions in the Rural Tourism. 2nd International Conference *Tourism as a Meeting Ground of Cultures,* 4-6 September, 2006. Siofok. Hungary.

Fotiadis A. (2007). Cultural Interactions in the Rural Tourism.Edited by Rátz T. and Sárdi C. Intercultural Aspects of Tourism Development, Kodolányi János University College, Szekesfehervar, pp. 35-43.

Fotiadis A. and Michalkó G. (2007). Rural tourism stakeholders and their difference in approaches. *Atiner,* 3rd International Conference on Tourism, July 5-6, 2007. Athens, Greece.

Fotiadis A., Michalkó G. and Rátz T. (2007). Rural Milieu in the Focus of Tourism Marketing. International Conference *Advances in Tourism Economics,* 13-14 April, 2007. Vila Nova de Santo Andre, Portugal.

Kokkosis H. and Tsartas P. (2001). Sustainable Development of Tourism and the Environment. Kritiki Publications.

Lane B. (1994). What is rural tourism? *Journal of Sustainable Tourism.* Vol. 2. No ½, pp. 1-6.

Martin S. and M. Uysal (1990). An examination of the relationship between carrying capacity and the tourism lifecycle: Management and policy implications. *Journal of Environmental Management,* Vol. 31, pp. 327-333.

Mathieson A. and Wall G. (1982). Tourism: Economic, Physical, and Social Impacts. McAdam D., J. McCarthy and M. N. Zald eds. New York: Longman.

Milman. A.. and A. Pizam (1987). Social Impacts of Tourism on Central Florida.*Annals of Tourism Research,* Vol. 15, pp. 191–204.

Richards G. (1996). Production and Consumption of European Cultural Tourism.*Annals of Tourism Research,* Vol. 23, No. 2, pp. 261-283.

Romeril M. (1985). Tourism and the environment: towards a symbiotic relationship.*International Journal of Environmental Studies*, Vol. 25, No. 4, pp. 215-218.

Andres Sarasa, J.L., (2001). El désafío del turismo en espacio rural. Proceedings from IV Congreso Universidad y Empresa, Valencia, Spain, 2001.

Sharpley R. (2002). Rural tourism and the challenge of tourism diversification: the case of Cyprus. *Tourism Management*, Vol. 23, No. 3, pp. 233-244.

Smith D. and Krannich S. (1998). Tourism Dependence and Resident Attitudes. *Annals of Tourism Research*, Vol. 25, No 4, pp. 783-802.

Smith S. (1987). Farming Near Cities in a Biomadal Agriculture. W. Lockeretz ed., *Sustaining Agriculture near Cities*.

Smith V. (ed.) (1989). Hosts and Guests: The Anthropology of Tourism. Philadelphia: University of Pennsylvania Press.

Vanhove N. (1997) Mass tourism: Benefits and costs. In: Wahab S. and Pigram J. J. (eds): *Tourism Development and Growth - The Challenge of Sustainability*. London: Routledge, pp. 50-77.

Verbole A. (2000). Actors, Discourses and Interfaces of Rural Tourism Development at the Local Community Level in Slovenia: Social and Political Dimensions of the Rural Tourism Development Process. *Journal of Sustainable Tourism*, Vol. 8, No. 6. pp. 479-490.

Wyllie R. (2000). Tourism and Society. State College PA: Venture Publishing.

Index

I

J

K